ENGLISH EDUCATION AND THE QUESTION OF INDIAN NATIONALISM

ENGLISH EDUCATION AND THE QUESTION OF INDIAN NATIONALISM

A Perspective on the Vernacular

Santosh Dash

AAKAR

ENGLISH EDUCATION AND
THE QUESTION OF INDIAN NATIONALISM
Santosh Dash

First Published, 2009

ISBN 978-81-89833-65-7 (Pb)

Published by
AAKAR BOOKS
28 E Pocket IV, Mayur Vihar Phase I, Delhi-110 091
Phone : 011-2279 5505 Telefax : 011-2279 5641
aakarbooks@gmail.com; www.aakarbooks.com

Printed at
S.N. Printers
Sector 2, Bawana Industrial Area, Delhi 110 039

for

Nana and Bou

Contents

Acknowledgements

This book has grown out of my doctoral research at The Maharaja Sayajirao University of Baroda, Gujarat. I could never have completed this book if I had not got the intellectual and emotional support of my friends, colleagues and family.

First of all I would like to thank my thesis supervisor, Professor P.C. Kar for his able guidance and support. He was so kind as to have allowed me to pursue my ideas at my own pace and on my own terms.

Janaki Nair, Madhava Prasad, Susie Tharu and Vivek Dhareshwar read and discussed early drafts of my chapters at different points of time. Their comments have added much to the way I have conceived and articulated the central problematic of the book. I also thank Rimli Bhattacharya for providing valuable intellectual leads.

I have also benefitted from the stimulating ideas and discussions at the "Culture and Democracy" Workshop at Gwalior organized by Centre for Study of Social Sciences, Kolkata and the "Re-figuring Literary/Cultural Historiography" Seminar at CIEFL, Hyderabad. I thank Tapati Guha Thakurtha and Susie Tharu for inviting me to participate in these two significant seminars.

I express my gratitude to Sudhir Chandra who, out of his interest in my work, helped me to access the facilities at the Centre for Social Studies, Surat. I thank the Director of the Centre, Lancy Lobo for providing free accommodation at the Centre's Guest House while I was at the final stages of my writing.

I am grateful to the staff at Hansa Mehta Library, Vadodara; Centre for Social Studies Library at Surat; National Library, Kolkata; Ramesh Mohan Library, CIEFL, Hyderabad; Centre for Studies in Society and Culture Library, Bangalore and Savli College Library, Savli for their unfailing help and courtesy.

I would like to thank Mr. P.C. Upadhyay, Principal, Arts and Commerce College, Savli for granting me leave of absence at the final stage of my writing. I also thank my colleagues in the Department of English for ungrudgingly coping with the extra workload this entailed. Without these facilities, I could never have completed my research.

I have gained much from many hours of passionate discussion with my colleagues at Arts and Commerce College, Savli. I especially thank Jayadev Shukla, Rajesh Macwan, Rajesh Pandya, Lalita Jadav and Harinivas Tiwari for our group readings and discussions at the college library. My students at Lunavada and Savli have shaped this book in ways that I am just beginning to understand. The lessons that I have learned from them are hard to come by.

More than anything else, the day-to-day companionship and support of my friends have sustained my faith in my work and have made it worthwhile to pursue some of the ideas in the book. My research would not have moved the way it has done without the camaraderie of M.T. Ansari, Paroma Deb, Jayasree Kalathil, Pavan Kumar and V.B. Tharakeswar at Hyderabad and Jagdish Chandra, Vinod Chinnan, Chitra K.S., Shivaji K. Panikkar, Rashmimala Devi, K.P. Reji and S. Santhosh at Baroda.

The affection of my extended family has always cheered me. I thank Bunu Bhaina, Bhauja, Tuku, Luna, Chinu and Dipu for their encouragement. I also thank Raju and Rinku for their hospitality during my stay in Bangalore. I owe a special debt to Mama and Viraja who have always managed our home in ways that has allowed me time and space for work. I thank my daughters, Kathya and Manu for being so loving and so patient with whatever they thought I was doing.

Finally, I thank my wife, Deeptha for being such an intellectual and emotional support. Since she is in the same profession and teaches the same subject, this book has gained a lot out of the everydayness of living with her.

My sincere thanks also go to Mr. K.K. Saxena of Aakar Books who patiently pursued my thesis and finally got it out in book form.

I dedicate this book to my parents who wanted to see me as an English Teacher.

Santosh Dash

Introduction

The central premise of this book is that education was a major site of subject formation in colonial India and that it continues to be so after Independence. It was a site where fierce struggles were staged against colonial domination on the one hand and caste privileges on the other. The questions of language and education were at the heart of these conflicts. However, nationalist resistances, as they took shape under the circumstances of nineteenth-century colonial India, came to focus more on the aspect of "domination" by a colonial power than on the "privileges" of the native elites. The passionate debates around the question of language during this time came to shape the idea of education in very decisive ways. One of the arguments in this book is that the debates around the medium of instruction during the nationalist phase produced a triumphal form of the vernacular that not only set aside the question of caste but also consolidated a kind of vernacularism that only learnt to denounce English as an alienating and oppressive language. The roots of this nationalist vernacular imagination have gone so deep and its hold over our minds has become so naturalized that it seems almost impossible to imagine whether our vernacular languages and literatures have anything to do with the continuing of caste dominance in India today.

There has been such a heavy investment in the vernacular issue in terms of tradition, culture, civilization and literature that a rethinking of the issue appears very difficult. It seems almost banal to think of caste in the context of the vernacular. This book is part of an effort to reconceptualize the idea of the vernacular in a manner that would recognize that vernacularism, much like Orientalism and Anglicism, is part of a colonial legacy and that it is a site for the production of elite control and power over the cultural resources of the nation. My research has made me believe that a long and exclusive focus on the English–vernacular divide in mainstream India has kept our imagination under a vernacular siege and has equipped us inadequately to deal with fundamental questions relating to caste and access to education. The debate around the medium of instruction which the nationalists set up during the struggle for freedom now seems nothing more than a luxury of the elite, particularly at a time when the "lower" castes in our society are demanding an education in English for their children. In fact, caste critiques of education have reintroduced the question of differential access of various groups to education as a central concern. Drawing upon these caste critiques this book makes an effort towards finding a conceptual way out of the English/vernacular binary.

The language question in India is significantly tied to the question of the formation of the national elite. No matter whether education is in English or in the vernacular, it cultivates elitism and elitism in India has caste as one of its major constituents. The divide between an English and a vernacular elite, therefore, is at best facile or at worst a constructed one. In fact, what is shared across this elite divide are elements of caste and class which are more significant than any difference that one could perhaps propose between these two language elites in India. Education in India is therefore not merely a simple issue of pedagogy or medium of instruction but involves questions of caste and class. However, the relationship between English and the vernacular, especially in the context of a national education, continues to be caught in a reductive and formulaic binary. If we do not recognize the complicity of English and the vernacular in cultivating elitism in India, it would continue to stand in the way of a radical reconceptualization of education in the interest of social justice.

A study of English education in India would, therefore, involve not only the pedagogical aspect of language and literature but it would also necessarily deal with other related trends in the civil society. For example, a study of English education would need to take into account the question of the vernacular as seriously as the question of reservation. The benefit of working at multiple sites of our civil-social life is that it takes our research out of the boundaries drawn by a discipline and allows it to resonate with other related trends in contemporary life. In the 1990s when I started working on the question of English education and Indian nationalism, I felt inevitably drawn to the question of reservation which had then raised a storm in our national imagination. The discourse on "merit" and "competence" was growing louder and louder and was threatening to decentre the more crucial issues of access to education and the constitution of educational monopoly. I found caste to be at the centre of this national debate on education and I thought it would be productive to use it as a frame to read my material; it is through this process that my research began to take shape.

On August 7, 1990, the then Prime Minister of India, V.P. Singh had announced the implementation of the Mandal Commission recommendation. The proposed 27% reservations for Other Backward Classes in addition to the existing 22.5% reservations in Public Sector jobs and education for scheduled castes and tribes had sparked off violent protests by upper caste youth, largely in urban centres in mainly North India. Protests ranged from street cleaning to boot polishing and "the discourses deployed most significantly were those of Unrewarded Merit and Salvation of the Nation" (Tharu and Niranjana 97).

It was around the same time that a series of publications heralded what is now referred to as the Crisis of English Studies debates. Although there seems to be no obvious connection between the reservation policies of the Indian nation-state and the English studies debates, a part of the argument in the book is that we need to invent frameworks in which such connections become conceptually possible. Scholars have already observed that the crisis in English Departments is "a crisis in the making since the 1960s" and that it is enabled by nationalist struggles, the women's movement, the civil rights movement, immigration and so on (Niranjana 1998 127). This crisis, Niranjana contends, is crucially linked to critiques of liberal humanism and universalism emerging from both poststructuralism and anti-colonial critiques. Niranjana's subsequent analysis of the mesh between the anti-Mandal agitation and the crisis in English Studies shows how this crisis has emerged "from a specific historical conjuncture" and the way it is locked into "present-day cultural politics in India" (1998 128). For Gauri Viswanathan, as for Niranjana, the crisis debates are marked by "an urgency of rooting our critiques in the present historical and political situation, rather than treating issues of English pedagogy and criticism as somehow divorced from other related trends in Indian Education" (1993 30).

This book operates with the assumption that English has played a very powerful role in the formation of various aspects of life in India. In fact, the role of English in India easily exceeds its function as a language or a literature. English has become so much a part of our everyday life that those who learn it and those who do not are equally affected by it. In fact, it connects us to areas as diverse as language, politics, religion and economics. It is therefore necessary that we integrate the question of English into the various aspects of our civil-social life. This would help us to evolve a framework in which the crisis in the English Studies could be read as symptomatic of a larger societal crisis in India and not as a West-influenced or inspired crisis.

A part of the effort in this book, therefore, is to examine the linkages between education and the question of merit thrown up by the anti-Mandal agitation. Through a study of the various forms of institutionalization of English and vernacular education, I attempt to problematize the notion of merit as it circulates in India today. Higher education in India has been broadly conceptualized as either English or vernacular and has traditionally been dominated by the upper castes. With the anti-Mandal agitation, the caste aspect of education has become very conspicuous. In my attempt to understand the discourse of merit in contemporary India, I have followed two methodologies. On the one hand, I trace the history of English education in India, attempting to locate those moments when the idea of merit was being consolidated. In this I work against a linear narrative, emphasizing instead specific moments or events which may yield insights for an analysis of educational merit. On the other hand, I seek to explore the ways in which conventional binaries such as colonial/national, traditional/modern, English/vernacular so often employed to frame debates on education might be dismantled, thus enabling a more nuanced understanding of education in India. Since they resist operating in terms of these binaries, I draw upon caste critiques of education.

This book has four chapters, with each chapter further divided into sections. There is obviously no single theme which runs either through the chapters or through the various sections in a chapter. The titles to chapters and sections are indicators of the fragmented structure of the book. I have deliberately used such a method of research to see the kind of connections that these loose fragments of thought can conjure up in our minds. Since the idea of English permeates through a vast range of life in India, I thought it would be more productive to track its movement across a range of sites than to restrict it to the site of education alone. The result has been that this book on English has yielded insights into a variety of incidents and events whose meanings would not have been available within the disciplinary confines of English alone. My research has touched upon areas as far flung as language, religion and politics with English working as a meaningful point of departure. For example, it has allowed me to make connections between colonialism, caste society, Macaulay, vernacular literature, reservation policy and text book production.

I have begun by pointing out how, for the British East India Company, whose focus was on trade, there was very little scope for return from an investment made in the education of the natives. Nevertheless, certain colonial policies, such as the permanent settlement of land, had led to the decline of indigenous educational institutions as funds which used to come from landowners started shrinking with the colonial extraction of revenues. Besides, these structural transformations introduced by the British had a profound effect on the perceptions of dominant groups in the native society. My analysis in the first chapter shows how, in the wider contexts of colonial structures, both the British and the Indians were active agents in the introduction of English education in India. My contention is that the institutionalization of English in India cannot be read as a simple displacement of an indigenous system of education by a colonial one because this process involved many complex negotiations, contestations, and resistances by the native elite. I have raised the question of agency in the context of the colonial educational policy because it would make open the institutionalization process through which an alien system of education was internalized and appropriated by certain dominant groups in the native society who actively used it in order to consolidate their already existing power and status in the society.

In this context I have drawn on contemporary research to show how English literature was crucial in making English education acceptable to dominant groups in the native society. Working from my own discipline, I have argued that the strategic deployment of notions of universalism and humanism in nineteenth-century India went a long way in establishing the secular credentials of English literature among the natives. Through a selective reading of Matthew Arnold, I try to show how a liberal humanist ideology was invented and instituted in terms acceptable to the native elite and how Arnold's references to the Hindu ideal of "detachment" could be read as symptomatic of the various nineteenth-century British efforts to constitute literary studies in response to conditions both at home and in the colonies. Simultaneously, I suggest that the liberal humanist conception of literature was part of an aesthetics that hailed "permanent" and "eternal" human values. In this context, I have further pointed out how a universalist aesthetics came to be adopted as a prime criterion of good literature precisely at a time when the working class in England had produced a substantial body of literature raising the question of "class" in English society and when the native elites in India were weary of the effect that a Western model of education would have on their caste-based privileges.

By systematically tracking the elements of native agency through educational reports, I attempt to show how official policy on education was compromised on various occasions on account of the fear of native dissent. The British sought to organize a modern, secular system of education for the natives despite resistance from the missionaries. In this they were propelled by the nature of the colonial rule itself to manufacture native consent. The "modern" and "secular" form of education which they put together had to pass through the native gaze of caste. Therefore, I operate with the assumption that what came to be instituted as a modern and secular form of education under the British had the sanction of caste. For example, the case for female education was resolved only through due respect to the native principle of exclusion and, more important, within the limits of patriarchy. It is, therefore, arguable that Indian modernity, much like Indian secularism, has caste as one of its constituents. A part of my engagement in the first chapter is to show how education served as a key through which caste could de-traditionalize itself and assume marks of modernity, the possession of English being the most obvious one.

From around 1835 there was a sustained effort to shape institutions of learning on the lines of services required for the maintenance of the colonial state. This led to the formulation of a whole new set of competencies which needed to be organized at the level of schools. Although English was preferred over the vernacular, it was noticed that many students discontinued their education at primary and secondary level since they were unable to cope with an alien language. A mixed system of English and vernacular schools, therefore, became a part of the education policy. Efforts were made to organize vernacular education at the lower levels of the school system. The higher level of education was, of course, in English. Such an arrangement of English at the top and vernacular at the lower level of education led to a division of skills as "lower" and "higher" but it catered perfectly to the needs of the colonial state in India.

The English-vernacular-led education was found to be "efficient" and "feasible" in the context of native society, as it catered effectively to the needs of both the urban and rural areas. However, when the three metropolitan universities were set up in 1857, it became clear that the education system had no uniformity either in the standards that it followed or in the courses of studies it prescribed. It is only after the establishment of the three Provincial universities that attempts were made to bring uniformity in the system of education. It is at this point that the years of study became crucial to the way uniformity was enforced in the standards and levels of education. I argue that through a technical manipulation, whereby the idea of "class" was made to correspond with the year of study, the colonial state effectively erased all differences in syllabus, examination system and teaching practice. This official neutrality in the matters of education was supposed to ensure a fair and just system of admission, instruction and evaluation of students, irrespective of who they were and what their location was in terms of caste, community and gender. My interest in raising the question of standards and studies is to show how a system instituted to maintain uniformity produced a certain formal and bureaucratic notion of justice while it effectively erased questions of caste, community and gender which were/are crucial in terms of access to education. In fact, the origin of a discourse on merit and efficiency can be traced back to such a moment when questions of caste and community were rendered irrelevant on the basis of a "neutrality" observed in the process of admission, instruction and evaluation of students.

In the second chapter, I have tried to lay open the various ways in which the question of education has featured in the writings of both the colonialist and nationalist historians. A part my concern here has been to explore the possible reasons why education, whether English or vernacular, has featured so prominently in the historical accounts of Indian nationalism.

Some of the major themes associated with English education in India are the themes of democracy, modernity, secularism, nationalism, etc. It is generally argued that English-educated Indians took command over Western principles of political discourse, initiated the process of decolonization and led the nationalist movement.

Colonialist historiographers stress the point that in spite of a "common" education in English, the educated Indians remained divided on the lines of caste, community and religion. It was as if the destiny of English education remained unfulfilled in a colonial society on account of the educated Indians' inability to disengage themselves from traditional ties. Such a delineation of English education and English-educated Indians has serious implications for an understanding of Indian nationalism because in these accounts the development of nationalist consciousness in India fails to match up to the high ideals of nationalism in the west. Nationalist historiographers, on the other hand, locate instruments of change outside the system of colonial education. Their stress on indigenous learning certainly problematizes the nature and content of nationalist consciousness by describing it as the product of separate but complementary forms of Indian and Western knowledge. Even while nationalist historiographers attempt to write into the nation making project, the values and ideals of indigenous forms of learning, they also trace the limits of nationalist consciousness to the colonial circumstances in which it developed.

However, what is common to both colonialist and nationalist historiography is their elitist bias. The location of such an elitist bias by the Subaltern Studies historians has not only exposed the ideological character of historiography but has also rendered problematic the status assigned to both education and the educated elite in the nation-making project. Subaltern Studies historians have argued that the recovery of subaltern consciousness, written out of both colonialist and nationalist histories, would not only enlarge the understanding of the nationalist movement but would also serve to displace education as the privileged site of the production of nationalist consciousness.

Following the *Subaltern* emphasis on the marginal and the invisible, I have focused on caste critiques of education located alongside mainstream debates. By citing the case of B.R. Ambedkar, I have tried to show how the colonial education system produced effects that became increasingly contentious during the time of Independence. The issue of education acquired a new dimension on account of its entanglement with questions of nation, subject and citizenship. It became clear that the struggle over education is as much against the forces in the native society as it is against the colonial state. My contention is that the narratives of anti-colonial struggle cast the educational question in the form of a fight between a "foreign" and "indigenous" language; whereas caste critiques of education, which focused prominently on struggles within the native society, were directed against the monopoly of a certain caste, class and community over the resources of education. My reading of Ambedkar shows how certain crucial issues relating to education were neglected on account of an overemphasis on the issue of the vernacular and English in the mainstream. I argue that the relationship between English and vernacular is more collaborative than oppositional. In fact, the vernacular seems to be made almost in the image of English.

The question of caste which Ambedkar raised in the context of education opened up the question of merit and efficiency in a manner that has relevance even today. It is clear that the uncritical acceptance in mainstream nationalist thought of the presence of educational merit of a particular caste, class and community of people continues to have enormous effect on the question of representation in civil-social institutions. My reading of Ambedkar seeks to show that the native elite continues to take for granted the benefits that have accrued to it on account of continuing access to systems of education. The Mandal Commission Report and the elite reactions to caste-based reservations have not only highlighted the caste constituency of our education system but more importantly they have rendered problematic the notion of merit and efficiency upon which the elite constructs its claim to greater representation. An elite class that has grown into national leadership has availed all the benefits of education, no matter if it came through English or the vernacular. The lower classes are still struggling to arrive at the scene of education.

My effort in the third chapter has been to investigate why the nationalist demand for an education in the vernacular fails the very groups it tries to empower. This failure, I contend, exposes the limits of the nationalist position on the role of the vernacular. There is no doubt that the nationalists established the national-popular image of the vernacular by articulating its value against the visibly alien character of the English language. The nationalist vernacular argument was meant to show how a separation of education and life takes place on account of educational instruction through an alien tongue. However, I claim that the nationalist projection of the vernacular as "popular" needs to be viewed in the context of its politics rather than as a democratization of the linguistic field. I further argue that the vernacular which came to be a significant part of the national educational system was of a deeply Sanskritized variety and was, indeed, as alienating as English.

Through my reading of an 1867 demand for a vernacular university, I have shown how an argument was made for the first time to impart higher education in the vernacular and how difficult it was at that point to identify a language that would serve as the vernacular of a particular province. In this context, I have looked at Sister Nivedita's formulation of a national education project in order to see how the development of the vernacular is imagined and how the proposed vernacular is situated in relation to a diverse linguistic culture in India. It is clear that Nivedita proposes the vernacular of a Sanskritized type as a means of release from the hegemony of the Sanskrit on the one hand and the fear of English on the other. However, my concern here has been to see the manner in which the Sanskritizing impulse emerges in the vernacular and how the Sanskritized vernacular is put up as a model for the development of languages in India with little consideration to the aspect of diversity. In this chapter I have also engaged with a late nineteenth-century Gujarati poet, Narsinhrao in order to understand the complex mediations which were underway in putting together a vernacular aesthetics around the lyric form. Through a reading of his engagement with British Romanticism, I have argued that the form which settles down in the vernacular as lyric is bereft of its history and is defined in a language borrowed from a high tradition of Sanskrit aesthetics. Here, I further show how a vernacular aesthetics articulated in religio-spiritual terms marks the literary away from the political while keeping it tightly under the grip of the religious.

My reading of a contemporary Dalitbahujan thinker, Kancha Ilaiah alongside Tagore in the third chapter is meant to demonstrate how it is no longer enough to think of the English–vernacular relationship in terms of an alien/native binary. Seen from the perspective of Dalitbahujan castes, it becomes clear that the Sanskritized vernacular which the nationalist elite advocated as a medium of instruction and as a means of literary expression thinking that it united life and education, has become as alienating as the English language. In contemporary India, if we are still committed to the need to integrate life with education, we certainly need to engage with the alienating effects that the vernacular has produced among people. I therefore argue that the continuation of an English-vernacular divide in post-Independence India only marks the continuation of a burden which we have acquired in our nationalist past, as a part of our anti-colonial struggle. The choice between English and vernacular makes little sense particularly in our time when caste critiques of the vernacular have pointed out to its alienating effects.

The last chapter of the book deals with the phenomenon of Compulsory English in independent India. Here, I draw my insights from my own location as a teacher of Compulsory English in a mofussil college. I argue that soon after Independence, the national mandate to commit education to the masses led to the democratization of education through the vernacular. Although English lost its competitive edge over the vernacular as a medium of instruction, it came to occupy an unassailable position in the vernacular system of education. The vernacular education, particularly at the higher level, was considered incomplete without English. It was in such a context that Compulsory English emerged as the most widely taught undergraduate course in India. My focus in this chapter has been to seek out the conceptual significance of such a course and to relate it to the political aspect of education in India. Stressing the need to recognize the pedagogical as political, I argue that a politico-conceptual engagement with the practices surrounding the teaching and learning of Compulsory English would not only extend the insights of the "crisis" debates in English Studies to English language teaching, but it would also work towards the production of caste, community and gender sensitive textbooks and teaching practices, which though inadequate in themselves, would certainly be a step in the direction of a more democratic education.

One

Colonial Education and Native Agency

SECTION I

WHAT IS ENGLISH LITERATURE?

My attempt in this chapter is to examine the processes central to the establishment of English education in India. These processes, I argue, have constituted English education in ways which continue to underwrite education in India today. In the first section I deal with the manner in which a liberal humanist ideology was lodged at the heart of modern, secular education. In the next section I focus on mid-nineteenth century educational reports to show the kind of alliances that were obtained between the colonial government and the native elite. Finally, I analyse key educational strategies which established and consolidated educational standards in the last quarter of the nineteenth century.

In this section I will explore the relationship between literature and ideology in order to show how study of literature is a politico-ideological activity and not merely an literary-aesthetic one. A literary-aesthetic approach operates with the assumption that literary works deal with universal human values and that the study of literature should engage with this "universal" aspect of literature and spread among people values which are true at all times and places. Instead, a politico-ideological reading of literature, I argue, calls for a more historically engaged reading of literature.

Working from my own discipline, I show how the study of English literature in colonial India was constituted by a universalist ideology that sought to eject the political and historical aspect of literature from the domain of English studies. What I have attempted here is a reconstruction of circumstances in which a body of writing came to represent "English Literature" and the terms in which they were sought to be studied in colonial India. I argue that there is nothing natural about the construction of a category called "English Literature" and that one needs to explore this category further for the sake of a more historically engaged understanding of literary studies in India. I, therefore, begin by asking the question: What is English literature? An exploration of this kind would come up against two basic queries: Why ask such a question now? Is it possible to ask such a question at all particularly when there is already a body of writing that is designated *as* English literature. Nevertheless, my attempt in this section of the book is to ask questions such as: What is the meaning of such a designation? and, whether the effect of putting together a body of writing under the name of "English literature" is merely literary-aesthetic or political-ideological.

There is doubtless the generally undisputed idea that an "English literature" exists; it is definable, recognizable, if not as one whose unity resides in the common national origins of its authors. In fact, in India there is still a tendency to associate English literature with British literature. We can't even imagine that this body of writing which we recognize as English Literature did not even exist a century and a half ago and that the study of English literature was instituted and formalized not in the country of its origin but in colonial India long before it became a part of the university curriculum in England.

A historical understanding of English, therefore, underscores the point that the study of English literature cannot be treated as a natural and innocent activity of reading and appreciating the literature of the English people, their lives, their culture, their values and ideals. Such a view, however, is still current in the institutions of English in post-Independence India. It is possible to teach, learn and take examinations and pass courses in English literature without acknowledging the conditions under which this subject came to be studied in colonial times and the circumstances in which it continues to be studied in postcolonial India. This is, of course, not to suggest that the teaching and learning of English literature has become irrelevant in independent India. Rather, it is to suggest that the pedagogy of English teaching continues to be treated as separate from the immediate socio-political history of our time and continues to be severed from the history of its beginnings. This could also be one of the reasons why "the much needed challenges to English studies currently being made in India seem not to have any identifiable reference point in recent Indian history, politics or sociology" (Viswanathan 1993 30).

Rajeswari Sunder Rajan has observed that the standard practices of teaching and learning of English literature in India entail a reading of more or less half a dozen canonical texts, which are explicated in the classroom and reproduced in the examinations with their authority derived from standard books on criticism produced by Western scholars (7). The English course is structured around a set of teaching practices that operate with the assumption that the teaching of literature has nothing to do with the mundane issues addressed by worldly subjects such as history, politics and sociology. The proper domain of literature, it is claimed, is that of aesthetics and ideas.[1] It is the domain of truth, culture and value and has nothing to do with the world of institutional structures and political forces. It is a domain free from history and ideology, pure almost to the point of being otherwordly. Such a view of literature is still current among the teachers and learners of English in India today.

There is, however, a need to understand the reason for the continuing power of such a view of literature even in the face of historical evidence that "introduction of English literature marks the effacement of a sordid history of colonialist expropriation behind European world dominance" (Viswanathan 1989 20). In fact, it seems as if the teaching of English literature in postcolonial India has successfully overcome the burden of a colonialist history of exploitation and oppression and has emerged triumphant without carrying any physical or material stains of that sordid history. Literature in our time, it seems, has asserted its essentially humanistic function as the repository of truth, culture and universal value. It appears that the rationality for the teaching of literature is to be sought not within the narrow confines of a history which is merely a hundred and fifty years old but in the eternal heart of mankind. In the words of Catherine Belsey, traditional literary studies have operated with the idea that "the sole inhabitant of the universe of Literature is Eternal Man" (1988 400).

There is no doubt that a certain notion of universality has come to be associated with the idea of literature and that it has become particularly forceful in postcolonial India. Such an association has also made it difficult for us to recognize literature as an instrument of ideology, of socio-political control. A combination of universalism and humanism has come to determine not only our ideas about literature but has also become an underlying principle of the entire education system in India. What is at the heart of the education system in India, Gayatri Chakravorty Spivak says, is the idea of a universal human being: "We were brought up in an education system [where] we were taught that if we could begin to approach an internalization of that universal human being, then we would be human" (1990 7). What Spivak suggests here, I believe, is that the education system in India offers basically a universalist education, no matter whether in the humanities or in the social sciences. The entire system is geared towards the enforcement of certain humanistic functions traditionally associated with literature—for example, the shaping of character, good conduct and, of course, love of humanity. Such an approach not only suppresses the issues of power, knowledge, justice, struggle and inequality but also constructs a master narrative of "people", of "mankind" and of "Eternal Man". In principle, one could outright reject all such essentialist and univeralist defences of literature, but it would be more productive to enquire into the interests that are protected when literature is defined on the basis of a universality overriding questions, for example, of "class" in England and "caste" in India.

One knows that literature in our time has come to be defined in two mutually exclusive terms. On one hand, it is characterized as a repository of knowledge that is universal and eternal, a characterization whereby the pedagogical aspect of teaching is defined away from the political. On the other hand, it is understood as an instrument of social and political control, an understanding that deepens the political meaning of the pedagogical. Gauri Viswanathan's work *Masks of Conquest: Literary Studies and British Rule in India* (1989) is a case in point. This book examines at length the strategic manoeuverings that were required for the deployment of English literature for the exercise of colonial control and dominance. It has unravelled the limitations of a liberal humanist ideology which has naturalized itself not only in our institutions of English studies but has also become a major part of our education system. Viswanathan has shown how English literature as a major component of our colonial education system facilitated the consolidation of a liberal humanist ideology. Further, she demonstrates how such an ideology crumbled under its own weight when a contradiction emerged between social control and social advancement "interest" in the colonial education project. The framework which she uses sufficiently explains the reasons for the gradual native disenchantment with the value of English literature. It also explains a similar disenchantment with liberal humanist ideology. Although it does not attempt to explain the reasons for the continuation of a liberal humanist ideology in the postcolonial institutions of our education system, it offers valuable insights for efforts to understand the complex forces that made for the continuing presence of that ideology.

After Viswanathan, it has become commonplace to argue that the introduction of English literature was a strategic move by our colonial rulers to invest authority in literary texts and to relegate social and historical questions to the background. This effort to divorce the material world from the world of ideas had already been made in nineteenth-century England.[3] Matthew Arnold provides an exemplary case in this respect. He was the acknowledged representative of liberal humanism.

Indeed, it is claimed that "during much of the twentieth century the justification for a liberal arts education and for the maintenance and support of university humanities scholarship in general has tended to appeal to philosophies such as those of Matthew Arnold" (Bauman 81). It is equally possible to argue in the context of postcolonial India that the tradition of criticism exemplified by Arnold continues to shape, to use a phrase which Foucault uses in a different context, "what we are, what we think and what we do today" (Foucault 1984 32). The well-digested critical vocabularies of Romanticism of Matthew Arnold, F.R. Leavis or T.S. Eliot, says Suvir Kaul, "are taken as pre-discursive and self-evident, as belonging to no histories and staking no ideological positions: theirs are the virtues of universal concern and trans-historical and cultural meaning and value" (210). This tradition has taken such deep root in the institution of English studies in its day-to-day practices that it becomes imperative to understand the reasons for its continuing influence. Therefore it is through a study of Arnold's views on poetry and criticism that I propose to explore the reason for the continued interest we have in literature as a humanistic phenomenon as well as the need to break out of it.[4]

Discussing the objects of poetry, Arnold says, "they are actions; human actions possessing an inherent interest in themselves" (1864 3). He further says that "the most excellent actions are those which most powerfully appeal to the great primary affections: to those elementary feelings which subsist permanently in race, and which are independent of time" (1864 3). On the basis of such premises he could argue that "a great human action of a thousand years ago is more interesting than a smaller human action of today" (1864 4). He could also deride the domestic epics of his time on the ground that they "dealt with the details of modern life which pass daily under our eye" (1864 4).

Similarly, regarding the state of criticism in England, Arnold says:

> here people are particularly indisposed even to comprehend that without the free disinterested treatment of things, truth and highest

> culture are out of the question. So immersed are they in practical life, so accustomed to take all their notions from this life, and its processes, that they are apt to think that truth and culture themselves can be reached by the processes of this life, and that it is an impertinent singularity to think of reaching them in any other (1880 34).

The function of criticism, according to him, is "disinterestedness" which can be shown by

> keeping aloof from practice; by resolutely following the law of its own nature, which is to be a free play of mind on all subjects which it touches; by steadily refusing, to lend itself to any of those ulterior, political considerations about ideas which plenty of people will be sure to attach to them (1880 20).

These Arnoldian arguments about literature and criticism need to be read in the context of the rising working class literacy and power in mid-nineteenth century England. One could see that the logic of his argument clearly served to undermine the value of the cultural forms that working class literacy had taken in England. Further, this logic worked by way of advancing a definition of literature in terms of "high seriousness". It is also clear that Arnold's logic was deeply entangled with social and political issues back at home as well as in the colonies and that his concerns in his critical writings are indicative of the complex negotiations that were underway between the imperialists on the one hand and the British working class and the colonies on the other. It is instructive to see the way Arnold sets up the notion of disinterestedness in his essay "The Function of Criticism in the Present Time". His notion of disinterestedness is precisely the one which allows the systematic downgradation of the politically loaded cultural production of the working classes. The notion is set up, curiously, in terms of "the Indian virtue of detachment and abandoning the sphere of practical life" (1880 33).

Even if it does not concern us to speculate about this reference to the Indian virtue of detachment and its possible implications for the working class education in England, it might be productive to ask what were the historical, political, literary and cultural conditions that made this reference possible in the first place. In other words, does this obvious spatial reference have also a temporal dimension?

Arnold's reference to the Indian virtue is neither accidental nor innocent. It is, by his own admission, quite consistent with the requirements of his time. He defines "the present time" in terms of England's colonial expansion. In such a time the notion of a national literature, Arnold argues, must take into account this fact of change in national life (1880 27). According to him, the best possible course which literary studies would take and which could be consistent with the epoch of expansion would be to recognize that "England is not all the world, much of the best that is known and thought in the world cannot be of English growth, must be foreign" (1880 41). Such an expansion of mind is possible only when "all danger of a hostile forcible pressure of foreign ideas upon our practices has long disappeared" (1880 27). To emerge out of a pressure of foreign ideas, according to Arnold, is to be released from the epoch of concentration.

Expansion, not concentration, should therefore be the rule of English literature and criticism. "Every critic," he says, "should try and possess one great literature, at least one besides his own; and the more unlike his own the better" (1880 42). However, Arnold's expansion logic which gestures towards cosmopolitanism shows its limits when his argument for spatial expansion is confronted with the temporal arrangement of knowledge and power across space. The future he could therefore envisage for poetry and criticism is the one in which Europe would be regarded "as being, for intellectual and spiritual purposes, one great confederation, bound to a joint action and working to a common result; and whose members have for their proper outfit, a knowledge of Greek, Roman and Eastern antiquity, and of one another" (1880 42).

What the above description makes clear is that words like "literature" and "criticism" do not have functions innate to them; functions are assigned. These functions are not only time and space specific but they also vary according to the arrangement of knowledge and power at any given point of time. For example, the moral and spiritual values that Arnold assigns to literature and criticism are only problematically located there and are in fact complicitous with the dynamic of power relations that are at work between the colonizer and the colonized. By defining literature away from "practical consideration" and by strategically aligning it with the ancient Indian virtue of detachment, Arnold establishes the authority of the English literary text in the moral and spiritual realm where both the colonizer and the colonized could sit and appreciate "the best that is known and thought in the world" while remaining completely detached from "a sordid history of colonialist expropriation and exploitation".

My suggestion is that such a conceptualization of literature not only fed into a European project of imperialism but also fitted into the caste and class aspirations of the native elite. Indeed, such an idea of literature was offered in terms acceptable to an already well-entrenched "learned" class of the natives who instantly recognized the value of the ancient Indian virtue of detachment as they saw in it not only the means of spiritual and moral progress but, more importantly, the confirmation of their cultural hegemony.

The rhetoric of spiritual and moral progress would have certainly sounded familiar to this "learned" class of the natives who thought themselves equal, sometimes even superior, to the colonizers in the "spiritual" and "moral" spheres. They willingly accepted the moral authority of the English literary text because, on the one hand, it did not pose any threat to the advancement of their caste/class interests and, on the other, it helped consolidate their "moral" and "spiritual" superiority over the rest of the natives who were not exposed to such literature.

What happened on account of such an exaltation of the status of the literary text in a colonial context, we are told by Terry Eagleton, is that it started a process whereby certain texts are severed from their social formations, defined as "literature" and bound and ranked together to constitute a series of "literary traditions" and interrogated to yield a set of ideologically presupposed responses (Eagleton 57). For example, Arnold's explicit intention in putting together a body of poems is that in having such "a collection like the present, with its succesion of celebrated names and celebrated poems, offers a good opportunity to us for resolutely endeavouring to make our estimates of poetry real" (Arnold 1852 88). The preparation of such a body of literature becomes an ideological imperative in the face of the recognition that

> an era is opening in which we are to see multitudes of a common sort of literature; that such readers do not want and could not relish anything better than such literature, and that to provide it is becoming a vast and profitable industry. Even if good literature entirely lost currency with the world, it would still be abundantly worthwhile to continue to enjoy it by oneself (Arnold 1853 89).

It is clear that what Arnold brought together as literature was a "collection" bound and ranked together with their "goodness" consisting only in their difference from "the mass of common sort of literature". Although the construction of "difference" on the basis of what Arnold calls "high seriousness" is arbitrary, this arbitrariness is not recognized as such since it formed a part of the dominant class ideology in England. Neither did it look arbitrary to the native elite in India since they always had access to high and serious texts in their own society. The point to be made here is that literature does not seem to have any pre-existing value, any "intrinsic, autochthonous, and universally recognizable characteristics" (Foucault 1977 22). It acquires value on the basis and manner of its deployment.

The idea that literature is distanced from material reality is not intrinsic to literature. But, it is precisely on the basis of such an idea that a unity is conferred, as is evident in Arnold, on a body of literary texts. Universalism is not an essential property of literature; it is only a characteristic conferred upon a body of literary texts. It is, in fact, possible to argue that the body of literary texts which we have come to recognize as "English literature" today is only a unity conferred upon it in the recent past. One cannot treat this unity as though it had existed throughout history with its identity intact.

It is therefore necessary to emphasize that literary texts acquired their universalist status in the context of colonialism. Literary texts that were studied in colonial India were not merely English in the sense of their geographical origin, a whole corpus of European literature was available in English translation for Indians. It might be of historical interest to explore the parameters that were used in selecting European works for English translation. It is therefore in the context of such a rearrangement of the world order that English literature was to emerge as representative of "the best that was known and thought in the world". Equally, it is necessary to recognize the authority and historical advantages which accrued to the English literary text on account of such a strategic deployment of the notion of universalism. What came to be recognized as literature or as worthy of being called literature was in fact a particular selection of texts chosen out of context and bound together for universal aesthetic consumption with little or no reference to the politics or history of the time. As I pointed out in my reading of Arnold, it is no longer possible to appreciate the ideals of literature and criticism held by Arnold without any reference to the native power relations in the colonies as well as the condition of working class people and their literature in nineteenth-century England. A critical and historical cross referencing of Arnold's principles of criticism in the context of the ideological requirement both in the colonies and in England would defintely move literature away from the domain of "high seriousness" to the domain of everyday politics.

This is not to deny the fact that literature had come to acquire an immense textual authority in the colonial context, both in England as well as in India. The textual authority was in no way limited to only the literary text; it was in fact available to texts on law, philosophy, science, religion and history. What appealed to natives, particularly the natives who were educated in English, was the idea of universality and equality which the English texts, whether literary or otherwise, revered. What remained at the centre of all their studies was the ideal of man which European Enlightenment thought had established as a measure of excellence in the domain of human discourse. However, it will suffice here to suggest that the English literary text, together with other texts on law, history, religion, had come to constitute a symbolic order to which the natives could appeal in case of difference of opinion with colonial authorities, particularly in literary, legal and religious matters. Together, all these texts came to signify modernity for the educated elite in colonial India. The elite among the native population who took initiative to reorganize their society in modern lines were divided in their opinion on what would constitute Indian modernity.

SECTION II
CASTE AND THE CONSENTING NATIVE

In this section, I will deal with the processes through which the native elite came to negotiate the question of education during the colonial rule and the extent to which caste remained a central point of reference in all colonial state intiatives in education. In colonial India the British had no option but to negotiate and engage the native elite on caste related issues in education. But, the common practice with historians concerned with education in India has been to represent native subjects as objects of manipulation and control by the colonial state. For example, B.K. Boman-Behram's book *Educational Controversies in India* (1946) is quite tellingly subtitled as *The Cultural Conquest of India under British Imperialism.* Early colonial initiatives in native education, according to Boman-Behram, was "an organized attempt to impose European civilization, chiefly through education" (*viii*). The British rulers who began with "tentative incursions", he tells us, picked their way "to certain working conclusions which has ever since governed the course and conduct of our education system" (*viii*). *English Education in India* (1976) by Kalyan K. Chatterjee declares in its Preface that "it was through generating a love for English literature and culture and the ideals Britain stood for, that the British sought to seal the imperial bonds. It is in this way that English education became an important part of empire making" (*x*).

It is evident from these prefatorial declarations that both the authors are methodologically predisposed to privilege the agency of the colonial state in their analysis of the educational process under colonial rule. The impression that one gets of the natives from these accounts is that they were devoid of all agency, without will or consciousness, excepting those imposed on them by the colonizer. The natives figure as poor, powerless objects, always at the receiving end of plans and proposals.

Such accounts of the colonial encounter where the colonizer emerges as omnipotent have been sufficiently problematized by postcolonial historians. These historians have argued that colonial hegemony was never totalizing; it was always incomplete and marked by indigenous resistance. The colonial penetration of the native community was never a one-way process. In fact, both the colonizer and the colonized were engaged in a series of negotiations over a complex range of issues which were never fully resolved either in favour of the colonized or of the colonizer. Therefore, the question of who was the active agent would only yield partial insights into the complexity of the issues over which there was a constant struggle.[5]

It is therefore necessary to desist from attempts to read the educational development during the colonial rule in terms of "cultural conquest" or "empire making". One limitation of traditional historigraphy is that it cannot properly assess the role that the natives played in moulding the colonial policy on education. My contention is that there was active participation by a group of natives belonging to a certain class/caste composition in the process of education. Any attempt to reconstruct native agency, therefore, needs to be sufficiently problematized through a simultaneous exploration of the caste/class nature of this agency. In this context, it could be productive to inquire into the relationship between education and native social hierarchy. Such an inquiry would involve two basic questions: one involving the colonial elite—what was the immediate past which the British referred to when they contemplated on a course of education for the natives? The other involving the native elite: what caste and class of people in the native community acted upon the prospects of a colonial education?

It is clear that the education of the native masses was not a part of the initial agenda of the colonial state in India. In fact, mass education was not a part of state responsibility even in England until the 1870s. There was a feeling in official colonial circles that "if England could get on without a state organization, there seemed little reason to introduce one in India; and the Company was at first a trading rather than a ruling corporation" (Sharp 3). The necessity for involvement of the colonial state in native education came inevitably through material and administrative considerations. It was recognized, as early as in 1787, that a course of education was necessary in order to "establish mutual good faith and impress the minds of the natives with sentiments of esteem and respect for the British nation" (Sharp 4). The colonial state in 1807, however, had the experience of the educational activities of the missionaries whose "zeal outrunning their discretion had brought them into trouble" (Sharp 4). Proselytization had become a nagging issue. Indeed, the Court of Directors had sent a despatch in 1808 declaring "strict religious neutrality and refusing to lend authority to any attempt to propagate Christian religion" (Sharp 4).

The Company, therefore, while allocating funds for education in 1813, pursued a secular model of education which had been experimented with in England but which had been put aside by the combined effort of the aristocracy and the clergy. The Company's chief motivation in following a secular mode of education was, on the one hand, to avoid any interference in the existing system of religious instruction in India and, on the other, to curtail the increasing influence of the missionaries and Anglo-Indians who had become major beneficiaries of missionary education by the end of the eighteenth century.[6] However, this planned avoidance of religious instruction and of religious culture was noticed by the missionaries who saw in this secular official policy on education an expression of the British middle-class mercantile interests. The period that followed 1813 was full of many controversies. The more important of these controversies related to (1) the role of the state and of private enterprise that was chiefly missionary at the time; (2) the nature of education, whether religious or secular, to be pursued; (3) the type of education to be followed, whether Oriental learning through the medium of Sanskrit and Arabic, or Western education through the medium of English. The educational reports of this period reveal that the Company's decision-making process was dominated by the Orientalists who were often openly hostile to missionary efforts in the field of education as they feared that "proselytization" would work against the Company's trading interests by inflaming native passion (Ellenborough 133). The Company, therefore, preferred to set up either its own schools or to encourage those set up by non-Christians. Such an atmosphere was congenial to Orientalist activity.

The early Orientalist work of Nathaniel Halhead, Charles Wilkins, William Jones, H.T. Colebrooke and H.H. Wilson had already established a view of Indian society which was to have considerable consequence in the later development in native education. These Orientalist scholars were closely associated with the judicial affairs of the East India Company. Their daily contact with Indians in the courts had convinced them that the Indians were litiguous, given to corruption and forgery. The colonial context in which the Orientalists acquired knowledge also led to a marked disjuncture in what they studied about Hindus and their organizational skills and what they actually saw in the eighteenth and nineteenth-century India. Their study of Hindu scriptures in the company of brahmin scholars made them believe that Oriental learning consisted only in the learning of ancient Hindu scriptures and that the brahmins were the cultural centres of "Indian" society and hence their authority was absolute and acceptable to the society at large.

The burden of a textual view of the brahmins and of their well-ordered society had come to weigh heavily on the Orientalists who were struggling with the day-to-day realities of the Hindu society. However, they were able to rationalize what they saw as an inconsistent fact of history by describing the present state of the Hindus as a fall from a golden past—a past which they thought could be redeemed through the recovery of the Hindu law (Macaulay 114). Indian society, as a consequence, was seen to be operating on the basis of a set of rules which every Hindu followed. The colonial ambition was to ascertain these rules through a careful study of the Hindu

Dharmashastras. The Orientalist effort, therefore, was concentrated on the study of select Sanskrit legal treatises with a view to ascertaining the rules, customs and manners governing the Hindu society.[7] It was believed that Indians would be best governed under their own law rather than under an imported British law. The colonial motivation was to maintain the *status quo* which, as their research showed, consisted in the recovery and the maintenance of the brahminical order.

The tools and techniques through which such Orientalism was practised in official and administrative circles came under special attack by Christian missionaries. The early nineteenth century saw a large body of literature by missionaries who worked with vernacular languages. Their interest in the vernacular was driven by their need for translating the Bible and other European religious tracts. They disparaged the official Orientalist interest in the idea of a noble and dignified past of brahminical supremacy. Instead, they favoured the use of the vernaculars which the Orientalists had dismissed as "the vulgar tongues of the Hindus". Thus, the missionary view of India coming later than the Orientalist view provided not only a critique of Orientalism but also gave a new perspective on the vernacular languages in India.

The missionary interest in the vernaculars and in the improvement of the lot of the common man went beyond the mere translation of the Bible. Charles Grant articulated this special interest in mass education when he observed that "except a few Brahmins, who consider the concealment of their learning as part of their religion, the people were totally misled as to the system and phenomena of nature and their error in this branch of science may be more easily demonstrated to them" (84). Unlike the Orientalists who proceeded on their grand amelioration programme of revival and improvement, the missionaries were more interested in simple demonstrations of scientific facts in order to ward off superstitious belief among the natives.

Although the grand method adopted by the Orientalists and the simple methods adopted by the missionaries had similar effects in the sense that both confirmed the supremacy of Western science and helped describe the native world as the civilizational "other" of Europe, it is important to emphasize the difference in their operational logic. In contrast to the Orientalists, the missionary ambition to make knowledge available to the masses had two sources: first, they were convinced that in Hindu society knowledge has always been the privilege of a certain caste of people, the brahmins. And second, they, unlike the Orientalists, were committed to reform and change. They were concerned with changing the existing social structure rather than with maintaining the *status quo*. In fact, the difference in their orientation can be better understood by taking into account the differential nature of their social background.[8] The Orientalists were better educated and came from upper classes in Great Britain, whereas the missionaries, particularly the Baptists, came from lower orders in British society.

The missionary interest in the vernacular worked inevitably towards their ready acceptability among the native population, especially among the oppressed classes who saw in Christianity a possibility for social mobility. But Christianity, which offered a liberating space to the lower castes/classes soon came under attack mostly by caste Hindus who condemned the educational activities of the missionaries and charged them with attempts of forceful conversion.[9] Captain Stewart of the Church Missionary Society, who had established at Burdwan two vernacular schools in 1816, had to face stiff opposition, especially from brahmins. Reports were circulated among the natives that "it was his design to ship all the children to England" (Poddar 85). Further, the introduction of printed books into his schools caused a sense of alarm among the brahmins "who apprehended it was some plan for ensnaring their children and destroying their caste" (Poddar 85). The British official policy on the missionary activity was always cautious. Although Charles Grant made a major plea for missionary activity in India as early as in 1793, it was only with the Charter Act of 1813 that the missionaries got official permission to participate in the native education programme.

It was in the same Act that a provision was made and funds were allocated for the first time for "the revival and improvement of literature and the encouragement of the learned natives of India".[10]

It was perhaps for the first time that the official involvement in education coincided with the interest of the missionaries. But these interests were actually opposed to each other both in principle and in practice. Subsequent official intervention in the affairs of the missionary activity only confirmed the earlier government censorship of missionary publications and public preaching. In 1822 Mr. Carrey was instructed "to discontinue all religious tracts calculated to excite alarm as to our motives in the minds of the natives" (Sharp 6). The colonial state, by actively discouraging the use of sacred books was not only consolidating its secular credentials but was also effectively separating matters of native education from the processes of proselytisation.

The British official policy on native education was always acutely aware of the fact that "the Brahmins would counteract the object were they alarmed into contest" (Moira 26). Lord Moira, while giving expression to the British anxiety over the form and content of native education, pleaded in 1815 that for "the progress to be effectual, must be patient and silent; like every other beneficial change, it must rise out of the general sense of society, not be imposed upon it; and to produce that sense I know no mode but education" (26). Here, Lord Moira is, in fact, giving expression to what was to become a major concern of the colonial state: how to manufacture native consent, how to "open the minds of the rising generation by due instruction" and how to "give them a habit of reverencing the principles which the Christian doctrine enjoins without stimulating the parent into opposition by teaching on point adverse to their superstition" (Moira 25).

A similar line of argument also underlined the official thinking about female education. The education of girls was considered a State responsibility only in the 1850s. Earlier, female education was confined to only those households "who can afford the expense of entertaining special instructors at their own houses" (Halliday 59). Reporting on the functioning of his Native Female School (1840) in Calcutta, J.E.D. Bethune held that his inspiration chiefly came from two sources: from the success of government schools, and the predilection of respectable natives against sending their daughters to schools run by the government or the missionaries (55-56). There was a feeling in the official circles that "the scheme of female education is doubtless unpopular, and looked down upon by the mass, with fear and dread, whether Hindus or Mahomedans" (Littler 57). It was also pointed out that "suspicious, ill-disposed natives may consider it subservient in some degree to the views of proselytism" (Littler 57).

The Governor-General Dalhousie had to tread softly in the matter of female education. He advised that "precaution may be adopted by as close seclusion of the girls as the customs of the country may require" (in Halliday 59). However, in a private letter to his wife, he gave expression to a different view: "The degeneration of their women had been adhered to by Hindus and Mohammadans more tenaciously than any other customs, and the change will do more towards civilizing the body of society than anything else could effect" (62). A similar sentiment was expressed in the Council of Education, but it was couched carefully in terms acceptable and encouraging to "all the liberal and enlightened natives of India". The Council, while deliberating on the benefits of female education in India, reported in 1850:

> It is believed that this [female education] influence will be even greater if possible, in Eastern countries, where all the earliest and most lasting impressions of infancy and childhood are now produced and fostered by uneducated and superstitious mothers. The evil influence of the Zenana is, in very many instances, never eradicated; and much of the good learnt by a boy at school and college, is neutralized by the habits of his domestic circles, and the absence of educated companions for this hours of leisure and repose. Female education is known not to be opposed to any of the religious doctrines of the Hindus. Indeed, in the early days of her prosperity, Hindustan could boast of her learned and virtuous females; whose fame was as far as spread as [*sic*] that of any eminent European

> lady of ancient or modern times (*Report on Public Instruction* 60-61).

Such a report could be read as an early attempt by the colonial state to exercise control over the domestic spaces of the native community and to reaffirm the status of public institutions of learning. In fact, much of the force of the argument for female education came from the recognition that the effects of public learning are "neutralized by the habits of domestic circle". However, the successful commencement of female education among the children of respectable Hindus cannot merely be read as the triumphant entry of the colonial state into the inner recesses of native community. The proposals to open female schools came from the native managers who, following the example of Bethune, asked for schools at Ooterparah, Neebudhia, Sooksagar and Jessore (Bethune 54). From the instance cited above, it seems clear that negotiations for female education were made within the economy of the colonial modern. The issue of female education was resolved within the principles of neutrality and with due respect to the native feelings for female seclusion. What constituted the colonial economy was the motivation to establish female schools within the boundaries of native patriarchy: "English was to be taught *to those whose parents wished it*, all were to be instructed in Bengali and in plain and fancy work" (Bethune 52; emphasis added).

It is quite evident that the colonial state was propelled by the nature of the colonial rule itself to manufacture native consent. The General Committee of Public Instruction in their letter dated 18th August 1824 expressed their opinion that "In proposing the improvement of men's mind, it is first necessary to secure their conviction, that such improvement is desirable" (Harrington et al 95). The Committee derided the "Maulvis" and "Pandits" who, "satisfied with their own learning, are little inquisitive as to anything beyond it" (Harrington et al 95). But it had to contend with this well-entrenched class of learned natives whose influence it could hardly afford to lose. For example, the Committee of 1824 felt that the only way this class can be propitiated was "by placing the cultivation of Sanscrit and Arabic within their reach" (Harrington et al 95).

M.S. Howell describes the opinion of the Committee in favour of Orientalism as "one of the most unintelligible facts in the history of English education in India" (Sharp 80). Howell was, of course, referring to Raja Rammohan Roy's letter in 1823 to Lord Amherst which described Sanskrit language as "a lamentable check on the diffusion of knowledge" (100) and the Sanskrit system of education as "the best calculated to keep this country in darkness" (101). The year 1823 was indeed a revolutionary year because it marked the start of the English education movement in India. But, more importantly, it was precisely at this juncture that caste was dissociating itself from its traditional and conservative configuration and was acquiring a modern form. Rammohan Roy's systematic debunking of the Sanskrit system of education and his pleading for a more liberal and enlightened form of instruction constituted the manner in which caste was to emerge as a modern category under colonialism. It is precisely through a liberal and enlightened form of education that caste had to shed its traditional marks and take on the marks of modernity. It seemed a historical imperative for caste to deny its association with traditional brahminism so that it could comfortably be chanelled into possible modern forms of dominance available under colonialism, particularly through English education.

It was not just Sanskrit education, but even the question of vernacular education was subsequently resolved in a similar fashion. By 1852 it was well-established in the official reports that "the vernacular schools were a failure" (Richey 68). The 1840 report of Captain Candey, Superintendent of the Poona Sanskrit College held that "the medium through which the mass of the population must be instructed I humbly conceive must be their vernacular tongues" (Richey 2–3). Similarly, F. Boutros, who had made an inquiry in 1842 into "the system of Education most likely to be generally popular in Behar and the Upper Provinces," pointed out that the opinion of the inhabitants of Calcutta with respect to English education was different from what was available in other Indian cities. In his report he dwelt particularly on the possible causes which might have rendered "a knowledge of English particularly advantageous in Calcutta and comparatively unimportant in the Mofussil" (7). In the mofussil schools, he contended, "the pupils belong to the lower classes of society, and not only could not pay for their instruction, but are too poor to support themselves at the college until their education be completed. The first petty appointment they can get, in many instances not worth more than 8 or 10 Rupees *per mensem,* induces them to leave the college, when perhaps their knowledge of English is hardly sufficient to enable them to read any but the elementary class books which they have read in the school" (7). In his report he also suggested that the demand for English education was only concentrated in presidency towns like Calcutta and that it appealed only to the wealthy classes in the mofussil. He observed in conclusion that "From all the inquiries I have made among pandits and moulvies, there is apparently no objection whatever on their part to have the treasures of European knowledge communicated to them through vernacular class books, without any reference to their sacred languages." (8)

The mofussil argument in favour of vernacular education had little strength on two counts: one, there was a visible lack of vernacular class books, and, two, there was controversy over the availability of competent translators as well as the amount of time that would be required for translation work (Jervis 11; Perry 16). Apart from these two commonsensical arguments which worked indirectly against vernacular education and which contributed to much of the official indecision in this regard, the most potent factor which seemed to close off the vernacular issue were the Reports submitted by the vernacular schools (Kerr 68). The Collector of Nattore, for example, informed in 1846 that "[*a*] Native Gentleman who constructed the school-house, informed me that the institution was useless. They expressed deep regret that Government should support vernacular schools which they do not want, and withhold English schools of which they stand so much in need" (in Richey 68). Further, he went on to say how he was once crowded in the town of Nattore by a group of people who said that "they did not want government to teach them their own language, and they called upon me to substitute an English school in its stead, as without assistance of Government, instruction in English was unattainable" (in Richey 68).

What is significant about the Collector's report is the element of personal experience which obviously informs his dramatic account of the native demand for English schools, in mofussil places. But more significant in the report are its silences. For example, the report does not provide any clue to the caste/class/community background of the "native gentlemen" nor, in fact, of "the crowd" that is referred to. However, it is possible to construct the figure of this "native gentleman" as one of the "educational organizers" since he had reportedly constructed the school-house. It is also equally possible to speculate on the basis of the Report of F. Boutros that the "native gentlemen" who had showed a preference for English schools might have belonged to one of "the wealthy classes in the Mofussil". In fact, from around the middle of the nineteenth century a class of educational organizers had emerged who in conjunction with the British were establishing schools for native education.[11] In the context of Bengal, these organizers belonged to what came to be called a class of "Bhadralok", people of respectable families. John McGuire, in a study of the Bhadralok in Calcutta, has argued that "the Bhadralok cannot be seen as a fixed social group, but rather as an embodiment of changing sets of organic social relationships" (43). In an economy under direct colonial control in which there was little prospect for the release of forces of industrialization, this class was trying, according to Partha Chaterjee, "to achieve through education what was denied to the economy" (1998 11). Although such attempts were utterly anomalous, the process it had engendered nevertheless an enlarged and modernized caste system through a reconstitution of the education system. Such an education was meant to benefit, for example, the Brahmans, Rajputs, Baidyas and Kayasthas together. The differences among these Bhadraloks in terms of caste/class, of course, surfaced in the course of development of education in Bengal.[12]

By mid-nineteenth century it was established that "achievement" was possible only through education, particularly through English education. Reporting in 1840 on native perception of social mobility, Alexander Duff said, "They pursued us along the streets. They threw open the very doors of our Palankeens. In the most plaintive and pathetic strains they deplored their ignorance. They craved for English reading, English knowledge. They constantly appealed to the compassion of an 'Ingraji' or "Englishman" (in Poddar 91). The Bengali journal *Sudhakar* in its issue of Sept 7, 1833 pleaded that "the government should sow seeds, all over the country, of that type of learning which can remove the darkness of ignorance and make man fit for administration and other public activities. It is necessary to establish an English school for this purpose in every village" (in Poddar 92). Statistics between 1834 and 1835 of School Book Society showed that English books were more in demand then either Bengali, Sanskrit or Arabic books. It was on the basis of such a climate of opinion and hard facts that Macaulay in his Minute of 1835 could rationally argue that "The sale of Arabic and Sanskrit books during the last three years has not yielded quite one thousand rupees. In the meantime, the School Book Society is selling seven or eight thousand English volumes every year, and not only pays the expenses of printing but realizes a profit of twenty percent on its outlay" (114). One could see that a logic based on such solid utilitarian principles might have given force to Macaulay's English argument. Macaulay could boldly declare that "on all such subjects the state of the market is the decisive test" (113) and the "state of the market" was decidedly in favour of English education.

The natives perceived education as a possible career for social, political and economic improvement and this education was solely "English" in nature. A feeling among the natives that "they have wasted the best years of life in learning what procures for them neither bread nor respect" had become quite strong. Such a feeling was obviously concentrated among a particular section of the natives around whom these official reports were structured. Macaulay's Minute only confirmed it: "It was impossible for us with our limited means to attempt to educate the body of the people. We must at present do our best to form a class who may be interpreters between us and the millions whom we govern" (116). It is no wonder that this class was quick to see the opportunities that were opening up in the public sphere and therefore was preparing itself for a career in English.

Wood's Despatch of 1854 suggested that the system of education in English would supply the government with "natives" of intellectual fitness and moral integrity for public offices of all grades. It was expected that the natives would help operate the state machinery and thereby consolidate the authority of the colonial state. The Court of Directors in their letter to Government of India also declared on 13th September 1854 that "It is now most desirable that there should be a supply of well-educated young men to take part in the extensive public works which are, and will soon be, in course of execution" (*Extract* 129–130). It is evident from these official remarks that the colonial state perceived the course of native education primarily in terms of jobs in public offices. Equally, the natives also came to think of jobs not merely as careers in public life but as "rewards", as marks of their "intellectual fitness" and "moral integrity".

The offer of a career in public office was highly ambiguous so far as the Muslim community was concerned. The Muslims had been systematically discriminated against in all public services as they were held responsible for the rise of 1857 revolt. Such discrimination was nothing new. It was, in fact, in practice from the beginning of *Wahabi* movement which started in 1803 with a *fatwa* which declared India as *Darul Harb* ("a country of the enemy"). This movement had intensified the hostility between the Muslims and the British. Starting from the days of Cornwallis, the British administration had systematically undermined the status of the Muslims in public service. But this attitude was expressed openly after 1857. A Persian newspaper *Durbin*, dated 14th July 1869 reported:

> All sorts of employment, great and small, are being gradually snatched away from the Mohmmadans, and bestowed on men of other races, particularly Hindus. The government is bound to look upon all classes for its subjects with an equal eye, yet the time has

> now come when it publicly singles out the Mohammadans in its Gazettes for exclusion from official posts. Recently when several vacancies occurred in the office of the Sundarban Commissioner, that official, in advertising them in Government Gazette, stated that the appointment would be given to none but Hindus. In short, the Mohmmadans have now sunk so low, they are studiously kept out of it by government notifications (Hashmi 23).

However, the gradual release of public posts for native appointments came to coincide with the setting up of a notion of "merit and attainment". The traditional merit which consisted in a knowledge of Sanskrit grammar, Vedantic doctrines and *Nyaya Shastra* was substituted by a modern notion consisting of the knowledge of Mathematics, Natural Philosophy, Chemistry, Anatomy and other "useful" sciences. It is possible to state here that the modern notion of merit came to substitute the traditional brahminical notion. In this process, a certain caste/class/community began to shed its traditionalism and acquired the qualifications of modernity. The British official interest was also quite in tune with the caste/class interest of the natives (G.T. Marshall 255).

Macaulay thought of raising an English educated class whose ties with the colonial state would be occupational, commercial and compradorial. Instead, what emerged was an English educated caste which sought to erase caste affiliations in the public sphere precisely because that was to constitute its modernity. There is a need to emphasize this complicity between caste and modernity, particularly when their relationship is often represented as oppositional. In fact, the tendency to define modernity in terms outside caste can be located in the manner in which the colonial policy was negotiated and finalized in favour of an education in English. The history of English education in India can be read as a significant area where it is possible to trace the insertion of caste into modernity.

SECTION III
OF STANDARDS AND STUDIES

Lord Macaulay's Minute of 2nd February 1835 provided a

systematic and severe comment on the policy of education pursued by the British in India. Macaulay held that the native interest in Oriental Studies was only "the effect of our own system" (114). This interest was what "We have, by artificial means, called into being and nursed into strength" (114). He observed that the Oriental system of education based on the idea of bounties and premiums had become unsustainable:

> What we spend on the Arabic and Sanskrit colleges is not merely a dead loss to the cause of truth. It is bounty money paid to raise up champions of error. It goes to form a nest not merely of helpless place-hunters but of bigots prompted alike by passion and by interest to raise a cry against every useful scheme of education (114).

In order to provide strength to this argument, Macaulay cited the petition by several ex-students of the Sanskrit College against their learning which only made them acquainted with "Hindoo Literature and Science" and gave them only "certificates of proficiency" (113).

Macaulay suggests here that the gradual abolition of a certain notion of proficiency and of studies had reduced the students to a state where they had to "beg that they may be recommended to the Governor-General for places under the Government—not places of high dignity or emoulments, but such as may just enable them to exist" (113). This also gives an idea of the range of reforms that were being contemplated by the colonial government, particularly in its effort to reorganize the public space. Earlier, the major object of rearing, through stipends, a class of students in the Sanskrit and Arabic Government Colleges was to raise law pandits and maulvis for the courts. But Macaulay argued that "It would be manifestly absurd to educate the rising generation with a view to a state of things which we mean to alter before they reach manhood" (114–5). In fact, Lord William Bentinck had already started the process of depatronizing Sanskrit and Arabic learning by his order of 1835 which had suspended the provision for stipends in Sanskrit and Arabic colleges. In August 1836 the students of a Sanskrit College wrote a petition to Lord Auckland to restore the stipends and to "preserve the Hindu *Shastras* from sinking into oblivion" (146). Lord Auckland resolved the issue by drawing a distinction between stipends and scholarships. He said: "By the stipendary system I understand an undiscriminating payment of allowances to students to induce them to attend a place of instruction .... on the other hand, I hope that scholarships, limited in number, given for a limited time, to the best students, upon fair and severe competition, may be considered as amongst the best stimulants to emulation and learning" (147). The system of scholarship must have been an incentive to the best students and must have created severe competition among them. But it must equally have worked as a deterrent to all other students who earlier could at least hope to pursue their courses with the aid of stipends to work eventually as religious teachers or astrologers. Lord Auckland, however, had made it clear that "the knowledge which gains, for men, reputation and profit among the native community .... is not to be acquired at those colleges" (1839 161).

From around 1835 there was a sustained effort to shape institutions of learning in the lines of services required for the maintenance of the colonial state and its ever-increasing system of native supervision (Auckland 1839 157). In this effort the government had to actively ensure a public sphere of activity where the skills and methods of a European variety could be recognized and rewarded in terms of jobs, emoluments and opportunities. By 1839, it was recognized that the earlier system of education had produced only "a promiscuous crowd of English smatterers whose average period of schooling cannot, *by possibility*, fit them to be the regenerators of their country, yet for whose further and efficient prosecution of studies, so difficult and so alien to ordinary uses, there is no provision or inducement" (Auckland 1839 157; emphasis in the original). Serious rethinking was underway on the question of English education. A strong official line of thinking emerged around this time favouring "a 'higher' education in English" and debates were held on *"the means of an advanced and thorough education"* (Auckland 1839 157; emphasis in the original). Auckland considered the case of the vernacular to be weak since it had only "a limited series of works for the purposes of common instruction" (1839 157). He felt that the vernacular medium might be good enough for "the purposes of common instruction" but is would be insufficient for "an advanced and thorough education". It was further argued by some officials, on the basis of their experience in Bombay and Calcutta, that "the understanding of students have been thoroughly interested and roused" (Auckland 1839 157) after they were given courses in English. Lord Macaulay had also testified earlier to the fact that "there are in this very town [Calcutta] natives who are quite competent to discuss political or scientific questions with fluency and precision in the English language" (115). Thus, the idea of competency came to be constructed not only on the basis of the abilities of a particular section of the natives but was also significantly defined in terms of "fluency" and "precision" in the English language alone. A competent person was one who had "the ability to discuss political or scientific questions". Consequently, it led to the formulation of a whole new set of competencies which were organized only at a "higher" level of education in English. A "complete" education came to mean only an education in European literature, Philosophy and Science through the means of English language (Auckland 1839 157).

It was, however, acknowledged by Lord Auckland in 1839 that the offer of a "complete" education had few takers: "the wants and circumstances of our Indian population bring to our colleges so few who desire, or are able to receive from us the complete education, which it is our object to impart to them" (157). In the context of the colonial society it meant that only a select few who could rise above "the wants and circumstances of the Indian population" could have access to a complete education in English. Macaulay's proposed scheme that concentration of efforts at the higher level of education would raise a class of people who in turn would pass on the benefits of European knowledge to the masses failed to make much sense in the face of facts that had come up by 1842. It was observed that "many pupils leave the college long before they have attained a competent knowledge of English" (Boutros 10).

The subsequent policy on education evolved out of a responsibility for educating the "most numerous classes". It was recognized that by merely raising the standards of instruction of a few classes of people through an advanced English education would hardly solve the issue of mass education. But, as I have argued in the previous section, all institutions of education whether in cities or mofussil towns, were monopolized by a certain caste/class and community of people who were indifferent to the progress of the rest of the masses (Monteath 1867 125). It is no wonder then that the appeal for the vernacular as a mode of instruction had very little value or prospect for the "more numerous classes" who were already under the burden of the existing class/caste hierarchy in Hindu society. The government-run schools which were in principle open to all classes, paid little attention to the "wants and circumstances" of this "more numerous class". In fact, these schools were establishing a new set of distinctions in terms of language and education.

It is possible to argue that the vernacular argument went only to strengthen the aspirations and desires of a mofussil elite who were eagerly pursuing courses of education in order to avail themselves of the benefits of jobs at lower places of public administration. In 1839 Lord Auckland had declared that "the vernacular tongues, and not English, will be the future languages of the courts and the offices in the interior of the country" (160). Subsequently, it was increasingly argued in favour of the vernacular that "the simultaneous study of the Sciences through the vernacular, with the study of the English language from the first period of a pupil's attendance would render our college education more interesting to all the pupils" (Boutros 10). It was also proposed that "the first elements of Geography, Arithmetic, Geometry, Natural Philosophy, Political economy" (Boutros 10) should also form a part of the vernacular course. It was envisaged that such an early acquaintance with the first elements of European sciences in the vernacular tongues of the natives would not only arouse curiosity for further studies in English but would also equip them for jobs at lower levels in case of their discontinuance. This could be an explanation for the clamour for vernacular education during the 1830s and 1840s.

The idea which was prominent was that a vernacular acquaintance with the European sciences would at least create conditions of eligibility for posts in "the interior of the country" (Auckland 1839 160). The possibility of jobs in public offices centered around the knowledge of European sciences. These jobs were systematically cornered by both the English educated urban elite and the vernacular-educated mofussil elite. Besides, English education in the wider sense meant not merely education through English. It came to include even education in the vernacular because what was taught through the vernacular was in fact English knowledge. Similarly, vernacular education under the colonial rule did not mean the study of vernacular authors alone; it was rather a study of European sciences through the medium of the vernacular (Monteath 1862 57-58). In the early years of its articulation, the vernacular issue was confined to the debate over translation of select European literary, scientific texts, and there was hardly any effort or incentive for literary composition in the vernacular.

The interest and scope of a vernacular study was confined only to the incentives it offered in terms of jobs. The idea that the spread of English literature would form the literary tastes of the natives and that it would help them to fashion their vernacular literature did not quite materialize. In 1837, Mr. Hodgson, while comparing the condition of India with that of Europe, argued that "there is no reasonable ground to hope here for the same wide study of English Literature, and subsequent use of information acquired in it for the purposes of vernacular composition, as occurred in the different stages of European civilization with reference to Greek and Roman models from which that civilization was chiefly derived" (in Auckland 1839 158). The colonial rulers were unable to project English Literature as one of the classical languages of India. They were constrained by the circumstances of a colonial society which hardly could afford "the magnificient endowments and establishments and permanent inducements of all kinds by which a difficult and exotic learning [Latin] was at length effectually naturalized amongst us [Europeans]" (Auckland

1839 158). But what the colonial rulers did provide was the inducement to translate a host of Europeans works of both the literary and scientific variety.

It was believed that the vernacular languages could be made fit vehicles for the dissemination of modern European ideas and thoughts if only they could improve and modernize themselves by drawing heavily from the classical Indian languages, Sanskrit and Arabic. This English-vernacular-led education with a marked preference for the classical languages had considerable consequences for the state of literature in nineteenth-century India. It encouraged the natives to abandon what was a vibrant medieval tradition of vernacular literature (for example, *Bhakti*) in favour of a high tradition of Sanskrit invented by the British. Susie Tharu has shown how such a process of inducement instituted by the British only helped "an endorsement of upper-caste power" (1991 164).

The British pursued the English/vernacular-led education in alliance with the native elite, both locked in a grant-in-aid system. There were, of course, institutions established by missionaries and many indigenous schools. However, in their Despatch of 1854, the Home Government had wished that vernacular education be placed on a level "in point of importance with that of the instruction to be afforded through the medium of English language" (Monteath 1862 50). But, H. Woodrow, Inspector of Eastern Bengal, while reporting in 1859-60 on the state of vernacular education, affirmed that it had remained the same as in 1835 when Mr. Adam made his first report on the subject. Woodrow's Report could easily grace a page in a book by an anthropologist as far as his detailed account of the primitive methods and materials used in vernacular schools are concerned. For example, after giving a graphic description of how palm leaves, plantain leaves and sand trays are used for writing purposes, Woodrow observed:

> The boys squat on the ground usually in two lines without much order, and Guru sits on his heels on a low stool or a plank two feet square; frequently he has only a small mat. The richer boys bring to school everyday their own mats tucked under their arm. The poor boys have no mats. All the children made their own ink at

> home of rice water and charcoal or charred wood... . The inkstand is placed close to each boy's foot and is perpetually being upset. In the course of two or three hours, little boys set their faces and hands blackened all over with ink. Books are seldom, if ever, used and reading is not taught.... The greatest extent of study is to write out an application for appointment and some lines of praise of Doorga or Krishna, to make out a Bill and keep native accounts (in Monteath 1862 73-74).

It was not just British official opinion, even the opinion of a few native gentlemen came to confirm the primitive state of the village school and the village school master. A "native gentleman" reportedly said that "village teacher or *Gooroomahashy, generally* writes a good hand, knows how to cypher, and is perhaps versed in Zemindary accounts; but he is a disseminator of false Philosophy, wrong Grammar, and is a perfect ignoramus in Geography, History and all the rudimentary branches of study required in a good secular education" (in Monteath 1862 74; emphasis in the original).

It is precisely through such a systematic production of opinion that the colonial state could authorize itself with not only the possibility of replacing these primitive vernacular schools and schoolmasters but also could hope to modernize the very nature and content of vernacular education. One could see that in the context of vernacular education the motive for modernization and secularization formed a single process through which, it was thought, the "primitive state" of vernacular education could be overcome.

Woodrow attributed the reason for such a primitive state of vernacular education to the absence of influence either of the missionaries or of government. The government policy on secular education had put the missionaries on the defensive and had consequently provided a certain sense of respectability to the government schools and colleges. It was precisely through a careful construction of its modernizing and secularizing credentials that the colonial state hoped to centralize authority and penetrate education activities of natives, both in rural and urban areas. For example, in his resolution of 1844 Lord Hardinge had instructed the Committee of Public Instructions to hold examinations for issue of certificates of qualification for government services (in Hashmi 7-8). These examinations were subsequently conducted by the Committee but the subjects that were included in the examination were those which formed the curriculum of the government schools and colleges. These subjects were claimed to be of neutral character. But what happened as a consequence was that the subjects of study in mission schools having a religious character were rendered impractical in the context of the colonial public service system.

It is, however, important to emphasize here that the content of education in the government schools and colleges was not entirely secular. In fact, in 1853, Charles Trevelyan made the following statment before the Select Committee of House of Lords:

> The books of English literature which are ordinarily studied in Government seminaries, such as Milton, Locke, Bacon, Addison and Johnson are replete with allusions to the Bible, and frequent reference to the Bible is indispensably necessary in order to their being properly understood. The Bible is, accordingly, constantly referred by the teachers and students, in the course of their instruction and it is often found at the examinations that the young men have in this way and by reading the Bible out of school, acquired a considerable amount of Christian knowledge. There is no restriction whatever to prevent it. (in Hashmi 8)

It is evident from the above observation that the secular credentials of English literature were not ascertainable. Both the students and teachers had referred to the Bible. If the examination papers were any indication, then they certainly showed that both had in fact "read the Bible out of school". But, such an acquisition of Christian knowledge was different from any direct teaching of the Bible. It was as a scholarly interest in the network of allusions and references that the study of English literature had come to establish its secular credentials, however tenuous.

It was on account of its ambivalent positioning between the religious and the secular that English literature had made itself acceptable as a course of study and had come to be taught in Government schools with little resistance from the natives.

The introduction of English literature was also crucial from the perspective of colonial policy since it helped define as "secular" the nature and content of education offered by the colonial state. It also impressed the native community with its declared intention to respect native religious feelings. More importantly, it made it difficult for the natives to make any easy association between English education and proselytisation. This was certainly a major achievement, considering the fact that the opinion of caste Hindus was against English education.

The colonial state was impelled by the nature of the colonial society itself to introduce courses of secular and neutral character. But in the process it managed to get active support from an influential class of the Hindu community who recognized in the policies of the government the protection of their own interests. In fact, the modernization and secularization process initiated by the colonial state had not threatened their traditional *status quo* in any significant way. It had only helped them to turn themselves into what Macaulay had called "a class of persons Indian in blood and colour, but English in tastes, in opinions, in morals and in intellect" (116).

It was through a careful construction of a series of beliefs especially among an influential class of the native community that the educational activity of the colonial state was put in motion. Wood's Despatch of 19th July 1854 had given sufficient indication that a vernacular/English-led education would be the most feasible one in the context of the native society. It was stated in the Despatch that not only the examinations should include subjects that are neutral but the same neutrality should be observed in regard to affiliation of schools and colleges (Monteath 1862 5). Subsequent to the Despatch of 1854 three Universities were established in 1857 in the Presidency towns of Calcutta, Bombay and Madras, and as per the direction of the Despatch they served as examining bodies on the lines of the London University. The universities were urged to "maintain such a standard as would afford a guarantee for high ability and valuable attainment" (Monteath 1862 5).

The principle that underlined the functioning of these

Universities was, to use a Foucauldian phrase, one of "embedding" or "the spatial nesting of hierarchized surveillance" (1979 170-71). The Universities became places of intense and continuous supervision. The Director of Public Instruction in each of the Provinces was asked to furnish reports regarding "the system of education established under orders of 1854, showing the practical results attained and the cost incurred by Government for them" (Monteath 1862 1). It was impossible to formulate an amalgamated report, considering that the growth, development and practices of education varied from one Province to another. But the reporting, however diverse, gave a certain visibility to the state of education in each Province and therefore legitimized the mode of surveillance.

It is less productive to try and understand the organization of education under colonial rule in terms of a "hidden agenda" which the British followed quietly without any public knowledge. Rather, it would be more productive to analyse colonial initiatives in public education as the effect of a power that consisted in its "open" and "visible" exercise. Such power, according to Foucault, "functions like a piece of machinery" (1979 177). It is a "relational power" and its functioning is that of "a network of relations from top to bottom, but also to a certain extent from bottom to top and laterally" (1979 176). If the reports that were submitted to the Secretary of State between 1860 and 1870 are any indication, they definitely showed that the entire network of supervision was carried out under three heads—direction, inspection and instruction.

By 1859, a series of establishments were already in place "by means of which the desired extension was to be given to the work of education" (Monteath 1862 3). An officer with the title of the Director of Public Instruction was appointed to each of the Presidencies and under these officers a staff of Inspectors and Sub Inspectors was organized (A.P. Howell 315 & 325). Such a mode of direction and inspection might give one a sense of hierarchy, but actually it was the apparatus that produced both power and agency. The expenditure on direction and inspection became a nagging point of discussion. But it was justified on the ground of "the necessity of keeping up a certain amount of controlling agency, however limited the sphere of its operation may be" (Monteath 1862 3).

The setting up of the three Universities had also considerable influence on the state of education. As is evident from the Education Report of 1859-60, the Universities were by then able to "infuse new life into our schools and colleges by awakening and keeping alive in them a spirit of generous and honourable rivalry" (Monteath 1862 11). In fact, admissions into the university degrees were in themselves very highly prized distinctions. The degrees were offered in Arts, Law, Medicine and Civil Engineering. However, a great deal of debate centred around the status of the subjects other than the Arts. For example, the status of a degree in Law became a subject of controversy. It was alleged that this novel degree of Law unknown in Europe offered only "a very humble standard of professional knowledge" (Monteath 1862 8). It was considered "injurious" and "suicidal" to the standard of university examinations. However, the issue was resolved with the realization that "it was both wise and right to utilize the examining powers of the university so as best to provide for the exigencies of the state and the public advantage" (Monteath 1862 8). Apart from the subject of Law, the nature and content of the course of studies in other subjects were also prescribed with the sole criterion that "they would provide tests of professional attainment conveying practical privilege" (Monteath 1862 8).

The entire school system was also organized around the same practical argument which had resolved the issue of subjects at the university level. The whole system was geared towards providing for "the exigencies of the state and the public advantage". For this purpose, the colonial state had to classify the native population into various groups and identify their specific needs and desires. The general classification of schools into "higher class", "middle class" and "lower class" more or less reflected not only the manner in which schools came to be distributed across space but also reflected the needs and desires of various groups of people. For example, a review of the

Educational Report of Bombay in 1870 showed how the Government offered "the elementary branch school for the day-labourers; the central village school for the villagers of higher station and aim; the middle class English schools for the residents in the large or small country-town; and the preparatory school and high schools for the student intended for college" (A.P. Howell 528). There were of course schools of ambiguous designation which did not fall within the neat divisions of either "higher", "middle", or "lower". This is evident from the various reports that were submitted between 1860 and 1870.

During 1862 and 1865 A.M. Monteath carried out exercises at the compilation of the statistics of schools at various Provinces. On both occasions, he expressed the view that it was almost impossible to "amalgamate" the various Provincial reports. In 1870 the same view was expressed by A.P. Howell who attributed this "impossibility" to the absence of any "uniform principle of classification and record" (524). Howell declared that "the absence of standards uniformly classified is the weakest point in our education system as a whole, owing probably to the education code [of 1854] containing no express provisions on the subject" (524). In this Report he included a special section called "Standards and Studies" in which he explored the possibility of establishing a uniform standard of education for all the provinces. His proposal reveals the centralizing tendency of the colonial state. It also constitutes an early articulation of a system of standards and studies that were proposed in order to legitimize the procedures of comparative statistics (of schools) and to systematize a whole range of data that were earlier considered "vague" and "indefinite".

Much of the vagueness of the data was due to the multiple use of the word "class". Sometimes it referred to the state of a school, whether Vernacular, Anglo-vernacular or English, sometimes it referred to the level of education offered in schools, such as lower classs, middle class and higher class schools. It also referred to quality of education acquired at a particular level. For example, as in first class, second class and third class.

One was a description of "class" in terms of the "medium" and "level" of instruction, the other was a description in terms of the "quality" of instruction offered in a school. Thus, the vagueness was on account of a mismatch between the medium of instruction and the quality of instruction offered in schools. It was, therefore, impossible to compare the state of education in various provinces and even within one province, unless a way was found whereby the mismatch between the medium and quality of instruction was corrected. This was possible only by devising a new way of describing "class" which would be both medium-neutral and quality-neutral. It was through the establishment of such a neutral description of "class" that it was thought possible to order the standards of schools in a uniform manner.

It was generally agreed upon in all the Provinces that the entire course of education from the beginning to matriculation should be a ten-year course. It was, therefore, proposed that ten standards should be adopted, each standard representing one course and each standard and each course representing a class. Admission to each class, except the first or lowest, was allowed only by passing the curriculum of the previous class. It was also proposed that "in primary schools, we should have a first, second and third class corresponding with the first, second and third years of study; in middle schools, we should have the fourth, fifth and sixth classes similarly corresponding with the years of study, and in high schools the seventh, eighth, and ninth classes on the same principle; one year in the ninth class qualifying the pupil to go up for the entrance examination in the tenth year" (A.P. Howell 525). Such a scheme meant that the expression "class" would mean nothing but the year of study. This was thought to be useful as it made it easy to locate the standard of a student doing his fifth class in any of the Provinces, in a mofussil or a city. For example, if a student was in the second class in middle school, it meant that he had attained a standard of study which a pupil would have attained after study for five years.

The system looks so simple and so familiar to us in postcolonial India that we wonder if it did not always exist. In fact, such a system was put together with the help of the improved methods of comparative statistics. A.P. Howell argued that "there need be no uniformity in the actual subjects of instruction; all that is wanted is uniformity in the standards embracing such subjects. There might be an upper, lower and possibly even a middle division of each class; but the broad principle of classification would not be affected" (525). It was necessary from the perspective of comparative statistics to maintain "a broad principle of classification" in order to ensure greater transparancy and uniformity in standards and studies across the Provinces. What was required was uniformity neither of subjects nor of mediums of instruction because that would amount to "interfering with the full discretion of the local departments as to details" (A.P. Howell 524). Instead, what was achieved through sheer technical sophistry was a highly monolithic idea of an "Indian" classroom.

The homogeneity of the Indian classroom consisted not in the uniformity of syllabuses, examination systems and teaching practices but was the product of a technical manipulation whereby the idea of "class" was made to correspond with the year of study. Such a neutral description of class was meant to ensure not only a comprehensive system of education throughout the Provinces but also purported to give a fair and just system of admission, instruction and evaluation, irrespective of who the students were and what their locations were in terms of caste, community and gender. In fact, the construction of a monolithic Indian classroom remains dependent on the uniform production of standards and on the efficiency of the system to measure and maintain the standards set for each class. By instituting a system of measurement that evaluated the quality of students on the basis of their preformance at a particular level of study, the colonial state thought that it had instituted a fair system of assessment. In such a system of education, the question of social standing of the performer had no meaning. What it had ensured was a universal and uniform system of studies and evaluation across the Provinces with the tacit assumption that question of caste, community and gender had no bearing on the level of performance and that quality, read merit, is the only criterion of education. Such a system of education, however, had enormous effect on the perception of the elite in the native society. An elite class which grew up under the colonial system of education acquired the same assumptions on which the system was built. One could also see how the erasure of questions relating to class and caste under colonialism also meant a corresponding erasure of such questions out of the imaginary of the native elite.

Apart from instituting a sense of formal equality at the level of teaching and evaluation, the colonial state spent much thought and effort in determining a suitable content for education. In the colonial context, such a process involved, as Partha Chatterjee has argued, "not a mere replication of a course of instruction that might have been offered at British school or University... The emphasis clearly was on providing a general humanistic education" (1996 11). Infact, under the circumstances of colonial India, the form of education was no different from the content of education. It shaped the Indian elite in very decisive ways, no matter whether they had an English or vernacular education. In the following chapter, I will examine the role education played in constituting this elite through an analysis of different strands of historiography on India which have featured this elite class as central to the nation-making project. My attempt will also be to indicate the extent to which the caste and class nature of the elite was instrumental in producing the native social order under colonialism.

NOTES

1. For early articulation of such a view of literature, see V.K. Gokak, "Speech at the Plenary Session," in John Press, ed., *The Teaching of English Literature Overseas* (London: Methuen, 1963) 27–34.
2. For example, as late as in 2001, the required reading for the first year undergraduate English literature course at Maharaja Sayajirao University of Baroda includes R.J. Rees's essay "Why We Study Literature?" *English Literature: An Introduction for Foreign Readers,* (Madras: Macmillan, 1973) 1–19. It was also during the same time prescribed at the first year level in the undergraduate course in Special English offered by Gujarat

University, Ahmedabad. The essay offers a general account of the nature and functions of literature, arguing that "by studying literature we are in some sense making ourselves better people: literature in fact is something from which we get moral education" (13). Students at Gujarat University, as elsewhere, are assessed on the basis of their ability to answer questions such as "Write a note describing the functions performed by literature." (First Year B.A. Examination, English (Main Subject)–Paper I, Gujarat University, April 1998). This is in keeping with the general objectives of the course—to acquaint students with "the Definition and General Characteristics of literature" and with "functions of Literature and the reasons for studying Literature" (Teacher's Handbook, Gujarat University, 1993) 26. This would demonstrate the way the designing, teaching and evaluation of English literature courses are premised on a universalist idea of literature.

3. Those interested in the connection between liberal humanism and institutionalization of higher education may refer to Emily Bauman, "Re-dressing Colonial Discourse: Post-colonial Theory and the Humanist Project" in *Critical Quarterly,* 40.3 (1998): 79-89. For a more sustained account refer to Chris Baldick, *The Social Mission of English Criticism,* (Oxford: Clarendon, 1983).
4. In the subsequent reading of Arnold, I have focussed on the three essays which are perhaps the most frequently prescribed in undergraduate and graduate courses in India: "The Choice of Subjects in Poetry" (1853), "The Function of Criticism in the Present Time" (1864), and "The Study of Poetry" (1880). To underscore this point, I have used a textbook edition which has been reprinted several times–S. Ramaswami and V.S. Seturaman, eds., *The English Critical Tradition* Vol. II (Madras: Macmillan, 1978).
5. See, for example, the manner in which the concept "ambivalence" is developed and deployed in Homi Bhaba's *The Location of Culture* (London: Routledge, 1994).
6. For a more detailed account see Austin A D'Souza, *Anglo–Indian Education: A Study of Its Origins and Growth in Bengal upto 1960* (New Delhi: Oxford UP, 1976) 8–32.
7. For an account of the process of the consolidation of Sanskrit treatises into colonial law, see Lata Mani "The Production of an Official Discourse on Sati in Early Nineteenth Century Bengal", in *Europe and Its Others,* Vol. I, ed., Francis Barker et al (Colchester: University of Essex Press, 1985).

8. For a more detailed account, see Bernard Cohn, "Notes on the History of the Study of Indian Society and Culture," in *An Anthropologist Among the Historians and Other Essays* (New Delhi: Oxford UP, 1990) 136–171.
9. For an account of upper caste reaction to missionary education see O.P. Kejariwal, *The Asiatic Society of Bengal and the Discovery of India's Past, 1784-1838* (New Delhi: Oxford UP, 1988) 212–4.
10. Extract from East India Company Act of 1813, Section 43. Quoted in *Selections from Educational Records 1781-1839*, comp. and ed., H. Sharp. 1920 (New Delhi: National Archives of India, 1965) 22.
11. For a detailed account of the rise of educational entrepreneurship see Harold Gould, "Educational Structures and Political Processes in Faizabad District, Uttar Pradesh" in *Education and Politics in India*, eds., Susan Rudolph and Lloyd Rudolph (New Delhi: Oxford UP, 1972) 94–120.
12. For a detailed account of the construction of the Bengali *Bhadralok* and caste, see John McGuire, *The Making of a Colonial Mind: A Quantitative Study of the Bhadralok in Calcutta, 1857-1885* (Canberra: ANU, 1983) 42–72.

Two

The Making of the National Elite

SECTION I
REPRESENTING EDUCATION: HISTORY, POLITICS AND NATION

Histories of Indian education, particularly of the British period, have described the Western mode of education as the chief agent of change in India. Some of the major themes that are usually associated with the accounts of such a mode of education in India are the themes of modernity, democracy, secularism, nationalism and self-government. It is generally argued that English-educated Indians initiated a political discourse which inaugurated the process of decolonization leading to a vigorous nationalist movement and eventually to India's independence. One of the powerful articulations of such an argument in academic historiography could be found in David Kopf's *British Orientalism and the Bengal Renaissance* (1969). The book resolves the issue of cultural contact within a cause–effect framework, stressing the contribution of the British Orientalists who, according to him "both historicised the Indian past and stimulated a consciousness of history in the Indian intellectual" (275). According to Kopf, it was the Orientalists who transmitted a new sense of identity to Bengali intellectuals and enlarged their "capacity for rational goal setting", an instrumental process necessary for the development of a modern outlook (Kopf 275). It is evident from Kopf's observation that the formation of the Bengali-Indian identity, of rationality and of historical consciousness was the effect of India's encounter with the British Orientalists.

The earlier articulation of a similar argument could also be found in Bruce McCully's *English Education and the Origins of Indian Nationalism* (1942), a book that reveals in the title itself its author's methodological predispositions. The book explores the instrumental aspect of English education both in terms of consolidation and subversion of colonialism. It raises questions about how the natives used English as a subversive instrument, but by aligning it with the origins of Indian nationalism, McCully, like Kopf, valorizes the educational policies pursued by the British on the one hand and the system of values acquired by the Indian elite through these policies on the other.

Such a valorization of English education has come for severe criticism. Gauri Viswanathan, in *Masks of Conquest*, exposes how "by perceiving the effect of [English education] as an incidental rather than willed outcome, McCully frees himself from the obligation of having to determine the motive force of English education, as does Kopf from that of British Orientalism" (16). Such methodologies, Viswanathan argues, causes "the phenomenon of Indian nationalism to be interpreted as the product of an unmediated form of English thought, with the ideas of the Western liberal tradition seeming to seep into the Indian mind in a benignly osmotic fashion" (16). Such histories associate, at least implicitly, the West with modernity and India with tradition. They usually conjure up the image of the colonizer as superior in civilization and culture and as an agent of change in colonial society. One of the major assumptions of these historians is that the Indians who were educated in English and were trained in Western values abandoned traditional beliefs and pursued liberal democratic values to an extent that it subverted colonial authority.

These success stories of English education stress the importance of our political education under colonialism. Although one cannot deny the significant role that the schools, colleges and universities played in shaping the colonial mind, the problem with such accounts is that they seek to explain the process of change through a singular focus on the action and behaviour of the native elite. In what follows I attempt a geneology of educated Indian elite to show how this figure has so obstinately occupied the imaginary of the historian and how this figure has traversed across a whole lot of histories written on Indian nationalism.

In the context of the relationship between English education and Indian nationalism, Cambridge historians have done immense work. Writing in the early twentieth century but active even in the 1970s and 1980s, these historians were concerned with writing "new histories" which mapped the processes of change under colonialism. Their work on India focussed primarily on how public and national politics emerged out of the action of the elites at both the regional and national levels and on the way the elite negotiated with the institutions of self-government established by the colonial rulers. Cambridge histories are significant in their attempt to rethink the existing frameworks of colonial historiography. For example, while writing *The New Cambridge History of India* (1988) C.A. Bayly took note of the fact that "much of the historical writing on India since 1960 has been a persuasive attempt to argue the importance of regionalism: political, economic and cultural" (*ix*). His attempt was, therefore, to explore how the rich peasants at the local and regional level played "creative roles in the formation of regional cultures and economies" (206). The emergence of these peasants and their contribution to the national scene, Bayly contends, "should not be seen as an Indianized form of a native doctrine of national progress. This would be a mere substitute for the historiography of modernization and of triumphal westernization propogated by the old writers" (205). Instead, he shows how these rich peasants, organized around traditional factions and religious groups, broke down "the resistance of tribal and nomadic societies, annexed the labour of backward regions and often sub-ordinated more completely their low-caste underlings" (205-6). Bayly, further argues that the "Resistance movements throughout the nineteenth century were directed against more privileged groups of Indians as often as the British" (206). What determined, according to Bayly, the political behaviour of both the rural and the urban elite was mostly their race for influence, status and resources.

A similar argument is offered by Anil Seal, another Cambridge historian, in his exploration of the issue of competition and collaboration in late nineteenth-century India. Seal observes that "the imposition of colonial rule had meant a shuffling of the elites in British India; its continuance meant that they had to be continually reshuffled. Collaboration came and went; new allies and new enemies envenomed the rivalries inside the country" (343). The historiographical dispute, Seal says, about whether the spirit of the nationalist movement came from the Western educated or from an indigenous tradition of revolt seems to miss the point. According to Seal, "an educated man continued to belong to a caste and a community, and hence he tended to belong to organisation of both kinds, one based on common kinship and religious persuasion" (15). In tracing the genealogy of the educated Indian, he points out that a "mutation" occurred in Indian politics around the 1870s and 1880s when the Western-educated Indians turned from being collaborators into critics of the colonial regime. The educated Indians, he argues, displayed a "certain detachment from British purposes" (23) and started experimenting with "new methods of public expression which soon incurred the candid dislike of government" (23). Seal, however, complicates the division of interest between imperialists and nationalists by arguing that "if imperialism and nationalism have striven so typically against each other, part of the reason is that the aims for which they have worked had much in common" (351). In fact, in the context of a colonial society, the complicity of nationalism with imperialism was discernible in the manner in which nationalism "sought to conserve the standing of some of those elites which imperialism had earlier raised up or confirmed; at various times both have worked to win the support of the same allies" (351).

The educated elites began to develop connections wider than the ties of family, caste, religion or locality and these connections increased their chances of starting a movement with an all-India base. But Seal perceives an ambiguity in the native elite's impulse towards political unity (202). In spite of their membership in national and secular organizations, the native elite's loyalty to caste or community was conspicuous. Their larger political strivings were, in fact, expressions of their narrow local interests. If there was any clash of interest between one elite group and another, it was mostly with regard to their caste or community affiliations. The educated Indian elite, according to Seal, was a special kind in the sense that the groups and associations that it mobilized were usually based on "castes" (342). This according to Seal, is one of the reasons why the nationalist movement in India can hardly be explained in terms of "the genuine nationalisms of nineteenth century Europe" (342). The nationalist movement in India had features peculiar to itself. For example, the emergence of a caste elite and its role in leading an organization of national dimension can be understood better by developing "a conceptual system based on elites rather than on classes" (341). Such a view is quite consistent with Seal's perception that the nationalist movement was "not formed through the prompting of any class demand or as the consequence of any sharp changes in the social and economic structure of the country" (341).

The Cambridge historians, in spite of their disagreement on several issues, do have some common understanding of the development of the nationalist movement and the elite politics of the (English) educated Indians. They usually see the emergence of public and national politics in India as an "uneven" growth. They attribute this to two things: one, to the uneven development of the social and economic structures under colonial rule and two, to the equally uneven penetration of education in colonial India. They try to break away from the models of Westernization and modernization by stressing that they are inadequate in understanding the complexity of developments in a colonial society. For example, P.J. Marshall declares that "whatever the ultimate significance of their rule, the British were by no means the only bringers of change" (2).

It is on the basis of such an argument that Marshall, in his history of Bengal between 1740 and 1828, can contend that the early British rule in Bengal cannot be understood in terms of "a chronology which is determined by the rise and firm establishment of a colonial regime" (2). Although the work of the Cambridge historians offers a rigorous reading of Indian history where change is not figured as a process attributable to the West alone, these historians continue to concentrate only on Western-educated Indians who gave some direction to an all-India movement. The questions that interested them were: Who were these modernizing men? Which parts of India did they come from? What were their relations with other groups in their society? What impelled them to form their associations, and from there how did they work towards a unified political demand? (Seal 23). From these questions it is apparent that these historians were methodologically constrained to take into account the identity-formation process of only the educated Indian elite and their alliances and associations. They could only argue that the elite and their alliances were "fragile", that there were internal rivalries between caste and caste, community and community and what seemed to confer unity on this otherwise uneven and disparate elite mobilizations was their Western education (Seal 23).

In his *Rhetoric and Ritual in Colonial India* (1991), Douglas E. Haynes has taken issue with the Cambridge historians on the question of Western education and its role in public culture. He acknowledges the formative influences of Western education on the Indian elite. He admits that the exposure to European political traditions was instrumental in generating liberal democratic ideals among the Western-educated Indian elite. But he contends that their education "must be considered a political process shared by the character of domination" (8). Educational institutions were certainly major sites of production of elite identity, but they were not the only sites. Further, the identity-formation *process* of the elite was not singular but multiple. The Western political discourse was a reference point, but "different elites selected different words and different colonial models from a larger potential repertoire" (15). Haynes shows that the Hindu elite's claim to be representatives of an undifferentiated local public and the Muslim elite's claim to be leaders of religious minorites were both "negotiatied versions of colonial political notions" (15).

In his study of the culture of politics in Surat city, Haynes shows how the liberal democratic values of Western origin "acquired very particular characteristics as a result of having been produced under colonial circumstances" (292). Tracking the politics of communalism and factionalism in the city, Haynes argues that they are not "remnants of traditional social patterns that will eventually be overcome by liberal values. Rather they are the products of the rhetorical and practical adaptations of indigenous leaderships to the needs of representative systems they have been 'granted' by their colonizer" (295). The suggestion he makes is that liberal-democratic ideals are contingent upon particular forms of domination and are not the natural outcome of universal human drives. The language of liberal democracy, according to Haynes, has become the monopoly of those who have many years of formal education in the European style. Since political discourse in India operated within the limits of an alien political idiom—an idiom unknown to many underprivileged people—it would be quite a test of democracy to see if these underprivileged groups are given access to the liberal order.

While the Cambridge historians argued that democratic discourse merely masked the true concerns of the dominant groups in India, Haynes shows how the liberal democratic ideals in fact produced forms of domination. Unlike the Cambridge historians who had treated liberal-democratic ideals as basically "western" and continued to use Western concepts such as "class", "bureaucracy", "capitalists", "aristocracy", etc. for their understanding of the Indian cultural and social forms,[1] Haynes argued that these liberal democratic ideals could be as oppressive in the West as anywhere. In fact, Haynes' idea is to "unravel the dominant western assumption that liberal democracy flows inevitably out of human nature, that it represents the culmination of the processes by which the world's people have sought to capture a voice in making their political environment" (296).

In their study of the movement of liberal democratic ideals in colonial India the Cambridge historians have persistently sought to show how their Western-educated followers used them to "hide" their caste and community aspirations. Therefore, what they read in the nationalist movement in India was "a vast swell of aspirations and rivalry" (Seal 351) against which the ideals of liberal democracy proved weak and fragile. Haynes, instead, acknowledges not only the strength of the liberal democratic ideals and the various oppressive forms it has taken in India but also sees "the possibility that cultural order may yet develop that [will] provide greater scope for social justice and for a genuinely democratic participation in the shaping of the policial world" (296). Haynes' optimism issues out of his recognition that "it is men and women who give shape to their culture, not the larger structures in which they live" (296).

One can see that Haynes' hope for democracy in India is articulated within the limits of a liberal democratic framework which he finds insufficient in its existing form. Such an articulation is made possible on account of a theoretical assumption that Indian democracy has "grown out of a colonial context rather than out of demands from deeper within society" (Haynes 295). What, in fact, accounts for the insufficiency of Haynes' theoretical framework is his disengagement with "the demands from deeper within society". Since Haynes tries to understand the movement of democracy in India within a framework of "colonial domination" he takes little notice of the resistances that were made both against the British and the native elites. Haynes describes the role of the Western-educated elite in the anti-colonial movement as only an "all-too-creative adaptation by local politicians to their participation in a representative policy established from above" (294). What comes across in such an account is not only a larger-than-life picture of the educated elite but also a too-insistent, portrayal of elite creativity, elite adaptability.

Such elite-based colonialist historiography, as we saw in Kopf, McCully, the Cambridge historians and Haynes, relies on an over-emphasis on the historical significance of the Western-educated individual and on the Western ideas of democracy, secularism, liberty, representative polity and the nation-state. In such a historiography it is the Western-educated individual who emerges as the only agent of action, and consequently history gets reduced to a biography that highlights his achievements and interventions.

Nationalist historiography has taken note of these idealistic and reductionist versions of colonial history and has recognized the implications of such histories for post-Independence or postcolonial traditions of intellectual discourse. K.N. Panikkar, in his study of the various aspects of intellectual history of colonial India, has pleaded for a re-evaluation of "the generally accepted notion of a direct relationship between the western influence and intellectual commitment" (56). He particularly acknowledges a whole body of writing on nineteenth-century India which includes among others the works of J.N. Farquhar, R.C. Majumdar, Charles Heimsath and David Kopf. Most of their historical writing, according to Panikkar, deals with social reform movements and the rise of nationalism and traces changes in colonial society "directly to western influence on the Indian mind" (57). Panikkar also takes issue with the Marxist historiography of Asok Sen and Sumit Sarkar on the ground that their works only demonstrate "how politico-economic structures warped the intellectual developments" (62) but can not delineate how "intellectual perceptions and positions were arrived at" (62). The questions that Panikkar chooses to ask are: Who constituted intellectuals in colonial India? How did they come into being socially and intellectually? What funtions did they perform in the given social and political situation?

Panikkar's use of the word "intellectual" is quite expansive. It is "not limited to a handful of activists but comprised a large number of lesser known people engaged in the elaboration and dissemination of ideas" (63). The advantages of such a notion of the "intellectual" are enormous. In conventional descriptions, educational influences are usually taken as decisive for intellectual activity. But such descriptions, according to Panikkar, exclude "the role of social experience: how social factors mediate in the formation of intellectuals and the growth of consciousness" (64). By including "a large number of lesser known people" with social experience but without any educational influence in his description of the "intellectual", Panikkar hopes to displace education as a privileged site of production of cognitive ability. Further, he distinguishes two broad categories of educated intellectuals: one nurtured only on traditional knowledge, and the other on a combination of the Western and the traditional. In the first group he includes Radhakanta Deb, Dayanand Saraswati and Narayana Guru, whereas the second group consists of Rammohan Roy, Vivekanand, Bal Gangadhar Tilak and Jawaharlal Nehru. After a careful perusal of the biographical information on these intellectuals, Panikkar concludes that "differences in the nature of formative educational influences did not prevent an identical mediation in the social process" (69). He also shows how "similarity in intellectual influences did not lead to identical cognitive ability or social mediation" (69). What integrated this group of intellectuals reared on varied intellectual traditions, according to Panikkar, was their "commonly shared socio-political endeavours" and their "common objective of social regeneration" (87). What these intellectuals created in the process was "the ideological base of a modern society, distinct from the traditional and colonial" (56). The problem with acccepting such a framework for an understanding of intellectual discourse in colonial India is that its application to the analysis of issues such as *sati*, Anti-conversion Petition, or widow-remarriage is predictable and formulaic. It only remains to show, for example, how these various problems which were organized on regional and caste lines were "perceived as common to all Hindus and (how) the intellectuals in three presidencies borrowed arguments and counter-arguments from one another" (93).

By making "social experience" and not just English education a crucial factor in intellectual growth, Panikkar questions the commonly held assumption that the cultural-intellectual struggles in colonial India were engendered though Western education. However, his valorization of the intellectual remains somewhat problematic.

The focus on the intellectual and on his exaggerated role in both early and late nationalist activity has been a point of discussion in the works of Sumit Sarkar. Sarkar's work *A Critique of Colonial India* (1985) provides a framework in which the role of the nineteenth-century intellectuals and reformers can be understood. Sarkar argues against any "overenthusiastic search for father-figures or precursors" (1985 70). Instead, he chooses to focus on the inadequacy of the historiographical models based on a tradition/modernity dichotomy in either describing the intellectuals or understanding "the specific logic of the colonial situation" (1985 vi). In constructing the logic of colonialism Sarkar shows how the colonial situation allowed voluntary consent, created faith in the good intentions of the British, gave birth to deep-seated liberal illusions and, above all, created a belief in English education as the sovereign panacea (1985 68). He proposes that it is only in such a context that the role of the intellectuals can be usefully understood. Their actions and their ideas, he maintains, need not be evaluated in terms of either their cognitive ability or cognitive failure. Rather, he says, "the limitations of our intellectuals, radical or conservative alike, were connected with the socio-economic structure moulded by colonialism" (1985 68). Indicating the various specific ways in which the colonial situation warped, hindered or frustrated the aspiration of intellectuals in the Bengal Renaissance, he demonstrates the way the "translation of Western ideals of nationalism, political democracy and social equality into *real movements* was far more difficult for the colonial intelligentia drawn overwhelmingly from upper castes, dependent for their jobs and often landed interests on the colonial structure and extremely distant from the masses" (1985 74).

Analysing the pro-peasant sympathies of Bengali intellectuals, particularly of Rammohan Roy and the Derozians, Sarkar shows how the pro-ryot changes in the Rent Bill and the Tenancy Act of 1885 which removed all restrictions on sub-letting of land were achieved through the organization of peasant meetings and Rent Unions. But he also shows how the breakthrough made in the Rent Bill and Tenancy Act was "of great help to ryots settled in Calcutta or other urban centers and enjoying occupancy rights over agricultural lands" (1985 65). These Acts were helpful only to those who had left the countryside and had come to settle in urban places with jobs acquired through their English education. Sarkar, however, does not reduce the occasional humanitarian sympathies of the intellectuals towards the peasants to some sort of failure on their part. He rather attributes it to the absence of any "agonized sense of alienation from the masses"—a sense of alienation which, according to Sarkar, would have "culminated in the going-to-the-people movement" (1985 67) but which was disallowed by the logic of colonialism. It was precisely this alienation from the masses that shaped the demands of progressive intellectuals—primarily Indianization of services and a measure of representative govenment—at least till 1905.

Sarkar's work on the national movement is set against the challenge posed by the Cambridge school historians. Sarkar argues that the focus of the Cambridge historians on elite aspirations and/or factional squabbles is "a kind of neo-imperialist onslaught" (1985 vi). Further, he says that the work of the Cambridge school maintains "a basically elitist stance with its incessant search for relatively privileged groups whose 'ambitions' are assumed to have 'created' political movements" (1985 77). Against this stance, Sarkar reads the national movement as a (failed?) moment which held a real possibility of mass movements inflecting/directing a leadership drawn essentially from the bourgeoise.

The national leadership, according to Sarkar, was as much under pressure from the bourgeoisie as "from below" (1985 vi). Through a careful analysis of popular movements such as "Tebhaga" in Bengal and the "Telengana" peasant movement in Hyderabad, he shows how, in contrast, these communist-led movements ended up in "self-defeating isolation in which guerilla war degenerated into sporadic individual terrorism" (1985 143). He further locates the limits and contradictions of communist leadership in its "policy of waiting on bourgeoise leaders and putting undeserved trust in their 'progressive' intentions" (1985 142). The significance of Indian independence, according to Sarkar, needs to be understood precisely within the limits and contradictions set up by the "inter-related labels of consciousness, both 'elite' and 'popular'" (1985 vii).

In exploring the relationship between popular movements and national leadership Sarkar draws on Antonio Gramsci's concept of " 'passive revolution': passive not in the sense of popular forces being inactive but, because the privileged groups in town and country were able to successfully detach attainment of political independence and unity from radical social change" (1985 143). Sarkar's "history from below" provides accounts of "Poor Peasants, sharecroppers, and agricultural labourers, labourers, often of low caste or tribal origin, [who] provided combustible material" (1985 143). This is consistent with his project of seeking to explore "popular consciousness" and not of discovering "popular autonomy". Sarkar's argument seems to be that popular peasant consciousness can only be captured in its relation to elite consciousness and that the "popular" and "elite" are not two distinct domains. The meaning of "autonomy", according to him, has to be located in their "interpenetration, mutual (though obviously unequal) conditioning, and, implicitly, common roots in a specific social formation. Otherwise the subaltern would logically always remain subaltern, except in the unlikely event of a literal inversion" (Sarkar 1997 70). His historiographical method is quite useful in so far as it explores, as it claims, the inter-related labels of popular and elite consciousness. But one could certainly ask: aren't we collapsing the questions of autonomy and dominance by choosing to describe the relationship between the elite and the subaltern as "obviously" unequal? Isn't the domain of the obvious precisely the domain of knowledge and power?

The question of autonomy and dominance and the study of their relationship have been major preoccupations with the group of historians whose practices from the core of a large body of writing known as *Subaltern Studies*.[2] The Subaltern historians begin with the recognition that "The elitism of modern Indian historigraphy is an oppressive fact resented by many others, students, teachers and writers like ourselves" (Guha 1982 7). Their project is directly related to the way history is taught, written, and consumed under colonial and post-colonial situations. According to Ranajit Guha, historiography, like literature, was one of the principal instruments of a "curricular effort to educate Indians in liberal values" (1989 309). Guha shows how colonialist historiography which began as mercantilist writing and a means to educate the servants of the East India Company soon developed into a "genre" of writing. In fact, the influence of colonialist historiography, Guha contends, had "so thoroughly permeated the indigenous historical imagination by the second half of the century that the British and Indian narratives of the history of the Raj were soon to acquire a family resemblance" (1989 308). Nationalist historiography which developed in "opposition" to colonialist practice showed a lot of "resemblance" to it.[3]

What is common to the colonialist and the nationalist historiography, the Subaltern historians contend, is their elitist bias. Both share "the prejudice that the making of the Indian nation and the development of the consciousness–nationalism–which informed this process, were exclusively or predominantly elite achievements" (Guha 1982 1). Guha, however, recognizes the "value" and the "use" of such historiography for those who seek "to understand the ideological character of historiography itself" (Guha 1982 3). Colonialist historiography, whose beginning Guha traces to the publication of James Mill's *History of British India* (1818) hardly spoke about India. Instead, Guha feels that Mill's history only "pretended to write the history of India while writing, in fact, the history of Britain in its South Asian career" (1989 291). Guha makes a similar observation with regard to nationalist historiography which purported to speak for the nation but ended up speaking only for the elite. The poverty of such historiography which spoke only for the elite, according to Guha, lay in its failure "to acknowledge, far less interpret, the contribution made by the people *on their own*, that is, *independently of the elite* to the making and development of this nationalism" (1982 3; emphasis in the original).

Guha calls the practice of such historiography "one-sided", "blinkered" and "unhistorical". What clearly is left out of this historiography is the *politics of the people*—a domain of politics which is "autonomous," for it "neither originated from elite politics nor did its existence depend on the latter" (1982 4). However, Guha's description of Subaltern politics in terms of "autonomy", "spontaneity", "consciousness" and "depth" should not be taken at their face value. His statement on the "autonomy" of Subaltern politics as well as his location of "a structural dichotomy" (1982 6) is not to emphasize that these two domains of subaltern and elite politics were "hermetically sealed off from each other and there was no contact between them" (1982 6). Instead, it is meant to show that a divergence of interest existed between Subaltern politics and the strategic and tactical politics of the various segments of the nationlist leadership.

It is not a part of Subaltern Studies agenda to break up the world into two opposing identities—the elite and the subaltern. The Subaltern historians do not seek a simple inversion of the importance given to the elites and their politics. Neither do they intend to valorize the political actions taken by the Subaltern classes.[4] Instead, their work seeks to expose the tendency both in colonialist and nationalist historiography "to contain all of politics within a single elitist domain" (Guha 1989 305). The inadequacy of elitist historiography, Guha contends, follows "directly from the narrow and partial view of politics to which it is committed by virtue of its class outlook" (1982 3). The consequences of such a class outlook in historiography, according to Guha, are enormous. On the one hand, such an outlook reduces political action to an "effect" of collaboration and competition between the ruling and indigenous elite. On the other hand, it excludes all popular action from the domain of politics and history "[when] nothing is left to politics but collaboration, resistance stands expurgated as an irrelevance and an elaboration without requiring further argument" (Guha 1989 300).

The Subaltern intervention, therefore, needs to be understood precisely in the context of "the narrow and partial view of politics" that underwrites much of colonialist and nationalist historiography. The parameters that traditional historiography uses to understand politics are those that "equate politics with the aggregation of activities and ideas of those who were directly involved" (Guha 1982 4). Instead, the Subaltern historian discerns two kinds of political "languages": the language characterizing the project of nation-building involving the rituals of the state, political representation, citizenship, citizen's rights, etc; and the language derived from power-relationships and ideological formations that pre-date colonialism. One is the privileged vocabulary of the Indian elite classes and constitutes a part of our colonial heritage, the other is the language which has very little to do with the language of citizen-politics: "that other language of politics, which is the politics of a nation without 'citizens'" (Chakrabarty 1985 376).

The two political languages and the two "contradictory" political cultures that they represent came to a sharp visibility with the coming of mass politics in modern India. Elite politics derived its language through the media and institutions of an English-style education. The Western-educated elites who read about the virtues of political culture in their English textbooks used the English idiom of rights and liberties in their anti-colonial struggle. Their politics, therefore, acquired a peaceful aspect as they pressed the colonial rulers "to match their administration to their own ideals" (Guha 1989 266). According to Guha, the educated middle class leadership took "the 'sacred' English idiom of rightful dissent too seriously for the [colonial] regime's comfort" (1989 267). The politics of the elite was thus bound within the legal and constitutional limits set by the colonial authorities. More important, these limits were not imposed on the elites, they were acquired by them systematically through English education. But the influence of their politics went only as far as the influence of English language and therefore had no mass appeal.

Partha Chatterjee has explored in great detail the difficulty which the liberal elite had to face in reconciling rationalist forms of an "enlightened" nationalist politics with the modes of thought characteristic of peasant consciousness. While concluding his masterly reading of Gandhism and its mass appeal, he says: "We get, in the historical effectivity of Gandhism as a whole, the conception of a national framework of politics in which the peasants are mobilized but do not participate, of a nation of which they are a part, but a nation-state from which they are forever distanced" (1986 125). It is precisely in this context that Chatterjee wants us to understand Nehru's observation that Gandhian politics bridged the gap between "the English educated class" and "the mass of the population".

Gandhi's intervention in the elite nationalist politics, no doubt, made it clear that an authentic national movement could only be built upon the support of the mass. It is possible to argue that this was the context in which the English-educated elite came to recognize the value of the vernacular languages for purposes of mass mobilization. Guha has shown how Gandhi invented a political idiom of mass appeal through a careful grafting of the Western liberal notions of liberty and citizenship onto the Hindu ideology of *Dharma,* identified as "*Satya*" (1989 269). The use of a dharmic idiom in the vernacular, no doubt, was useful in mobilizing the masses but, as Guha argues, it hardly proved the authority of *Satyagraha* theory itself. Recent research has also shown that popular mobilization during the nationalist struggle very often took violent forms which undermined the authority of *Satyagraha*.[5] Further, the expectations of the peasantry were in violent contradiction to the stated goals and methods of the nationalist leadership. The elite's recourse to the idiom of *dharma* was "to justify and explain the initiatives by which they hoped to make their subordinates relate to them as non-antagonistically as possible" (Guha 1989 244).

The dharmic idiom was expected, on the one hand, "to stop popular militancy from 'going too far' " and on the other, "to stop class struggle from boiling over into armed conflict" (Guha 1989 265). But, in the process the elite in its attempt to speak for the nation had come to "rely heavily on the traditional idiom of *Dharma,* with the curious result that something as contemporary as nineteenth-and-twentieth-century nationalism often made its appearance in political discourse dressed up as ancient Hindu wisdom" (Guha 1989 245). Further, an exclusive emphasis on Hindu *dharma*, Guha argues, "divided the nation, ranging peasantry against rural gentry, the Namsudras against upper castes, and above all, Muslims and Hindus against each other" (1989 246). The significance of such an argument is that it stops blaming colonialism for "all the uncomfortable aspects of popular mentality, such as 'casteism,' 'regionalism,' 'communalism' etc." Instead, it questions the category of the "nation" and poses the failure of the "nation" to come into its own as "a fundamental problem of modern Indian history" (Chakrabarty 1995 373).

It is clear from the above account of the recent historiography in/on India that descriptions of Indian nationalism significantly engaged with the relation between the popular and the elite. It is equally clear that the elite class which grew into the "national" leadership in the early decades of the twentieth century was significantly constituted by a modern education which enabled it to push for enhanced political power. This bid for political power was locked in with the question of mass mobilization, a question which in turn was tied to the idea of the vernacular as a mobilizing instrument. However, education in the vernacular was hardly different from "English" education as the vernacular came to be conceived within the confines of a caste imperative. (I will argue this point in the following chapter.) What the Subaltern perspective offers to the above understanding is that alongside mainstream debates on education, arguably a major site of elitist consolidation, powerful caste-based critiques of education were available in terms outside the colonial-national paradigm. These critiques might refigure our understanding of the relationship between the "popular" and the "elite" and might thereby allow us to rethink the question of English and the vernacular. In the following section, I will take up one such caste critique for analysis in order to show how the blindness about the caste question continues in contemporary India and how important it is to factor in caste as a quantity to be negotiated in all our nation-making projects. The modern secular education has led the Indian elite to believe that caste is no longer a contemporary issue. A revisit to the caste question through a caste critique of education might help us to reconfigure our priorities in the field of education.

SECTION II
AMBEDKAR AND A POSSIBLE CRITIQUE OF EDUCATION IN INDIA

Education has been at the heart of the nation-building project in India since 1947. The various Reports, Bills, Acts, formulas and policies adopted by the Indian government have always emphasized the centrality of the question of the "nation" to our education system. One example of such a document is the University Grants Commission (UGC) guidelines to universities in India asking for Seventh Plan Proposals.[6] The UGC document suggests that "development" should take place in the spirit of the National Education Policy of 1986. The most important aspect of the Policy, universities are told, is the realization that "education is a means of national development at all levels—economic, political and social and that the development plans of the universities should try to translate this realization into reality" (1). The immensity of the educational task for "national development" is further deepened with declarations such as:

(*a*) India's political and social life has got totally eroded and we are at the threshold of collapse of traditional values. It is the education system alone which can retrieve the situation in this regard. (4)

(*b*) In our culturally pluralistic society, education should foster universal and eternal values which are oriented towards the unity and integration of our poeple and should help eliminate obscurantism, religious fanaticism, violence, superstition and fatalism etc. (4)

(*c*) All educational programmes will be carried on in strict conformity with secular values. (5)

(*d*) There should be adequate educational opportunities for weaker sections, minorities etc. and, in fact, there should be education for all. (2)

The UGC document lists all that is desirable in the production of an enlightened and humane society. But one thing that has become clear in the last fifty years of policy-making is that there is a fragility at the very heart of the nation-building project. The visibility of such a fragile core is simultaneous with a crisis in civil society. Although it is easy to envisage, as the UGC document does, the movement of education in terms of "progress" and "development" it could perhaps be useful to read this movement as singularly undemocratic, especially in the wake of various contestations in the name of "language", "caste", "class", "community", "region", "religion", "gender" etc. In fact, the very idea of progress, as Antonio Gramsci has tellingly delineated, depends on "a specific mentality"; it implies "the possibility of quantitative and qualitative measuring, of "more" and "better"; it supposes a "fixed" or fixable yardstick—a yardstick which is "given by the past, by a certain phase of the past" (Gramsci 357). Thus, the question of defining the "nation", as indeed of "progress", in the present circumstances no longer remains as unproblematic as the UGC document assumes.

It is evident that the UGC document valorizes only a particular notion of the "nation" and offers it not only as being desirable but as being "natural" and "normal". The consequences of maintaining such a monolithic and unitary idea of the nation are enormous. Such an identity, by necessity, excludes contestatory elements and dismisses them as divisive and dangerous. For example, the diverse and pluralistic nature of the Indian society is emphasized in the UGC document, but it is quickly subverted. This subversion is naturalized in the name of "unity and integration of our people" (4). This has been consistent with the language of the nation since Independence. Some of the questions which need to be raised here are the following: What is the nature of this language which makes a subversion look so natural and normal? How is such a language constituted? What is it in the language of the nation that ensures the consistent and repetitive production of a flat and singular national identity?

There have been several moves in the recent past to dismantle the image of a unified nation. These moves have taken several shapes and have occurred across several practices. Within the academia the effort has been on critiquing the underlying logic of representations of unity.[7] There is a growing realization that our understanding of the nation has been consistently singular and that it has failed us historically, politically and, what is more important, conceptually. A singular concept of the "nation" has neglected and is still neglecting a powerful history which has grown and is still growing outside history as nation. Such an exclusionary representation of the nation has further led us into various impasses and aporias on account of its refusal to acknowledge, understand or engage with various other identities, claims, protests and contestations made beside "national" identity. What seems to have emerged today is the recognition that our national identity is predicated on an elite and pervasive agenda of nation-building. However, this elitism in the nation-building activity is now challenged by a set of rival definitions of the nation that are being made outside and against the avowed intentions of state policy.

The current visibility of a parallel history of rival definitions marks a highly self-conscious phase of our historical engagement with the question of the "nation". It is argued that the idea of the "nation" and "nationalism" can no longer be taken for granted. It is, no doubt, praiseworthy to bring patriotic sentiments to bear on the history of Indian nationalism, but such sentiments scarcely advance knowledge about our immediate past—a past which is increasingly becoming distant on account of our uncritical acceptance of the Indian nationhood.

It has been argued recently that "while the historical conjuncture in the west favoured a convergence between the nation and nationalism, it did not do so in the subcontinent. Nationalism here largely diverged from the nation and advanced towards the formation of a state-system" (Aloysius 226). What underlies such an argument is the idea that the Indian nationalism is historically comparable to the nationalisms of the West. In fact, there is a large body of work on Indian nationalism which operates precisely within such comparative frameworks, invariably producing eurocentric readings of nationalism. The various nationalisms of the West emerge, in these readings, as "progressive", "genuine", "ideal" and, above all, "political", as against subcontinental nationalism which is seen as "derivative", "reactionary" and at best, "cultural".

Partha Chatterjee, in *Nationalist Thought and The Colonial World: A Derivative Discourse?* (1986), has shown the inadequacy of such comparative models for the study of nationalism in India. He argues that it would be dogmatic to assert that Indian nationalism and "its logical principles and theoretical concepts are wholly derived from another framework of knowledge—that of modern Western rational thought" (1986 41). He does not suggest that there was no borrowing and that nationalist thought is exclusively culture specific. Instead, he argues that "nationalist thought is selective about what it takes from Western rational thought. Indeed, it is deliberately and necessarily selective. Its political burden, as we have said, is to oppose colonial rule" (1986 41). Chatterjee argues that there is a "historical" process through which nationalist discourse has constituted itself; it did not "simply 'emerge' out of a social structure or out of the supposedly objective workings of a world historical process" (1986 40) but was thought out, formulated, propagated and defended in the battlefield of politics.

What, therefore, needs to be explored, according to Chatterjee, is the process through which "a unity was established between nationalist thought and nationalist politics" (1986 40). He, of course, is aware that nationalist thought, even though it claimed for itself a certain unity and autonomy, was far from being monolithic. However, his project is not merely to contest the unity of the nationalist ideology, but to identify the "positive" aspect of this unity which seeks "to assert the feasibility of entirely new political possibilities" (1986 40). His attempt to study the nationalist ideology in terms of "unity" and "content" seems to be the outcome of such a project. He suggests that there is a relation between the content of nationalist discourse and the kind of politics which nationalism conducts. It is the content of the nationalist ideology, its claims about what is possible and what is legitimate which, according to Chatterjee, give "specific shape to its politics" (1986 40). A study of the politics and ideology of nationalism would, therefore, involve not only an exploration of the unity of nationalist thought and "the possibilities it seeks to actualize in the unified life of the state" (1986 51) but a process of showing "how some possibilities are emphasized, others erased, how the marks of disjuncture are suppressed and the rational continuity of a progressive historical development established" (1986 52).

What is particularly significant here is Chatterjee's suggestion that "the critical analysis of nationalist thought is also necessarily an intervention in the political discourse of our own time" (1986 52). In his engagement with the question of nation and nationalism Chatterjee poses the ideological creation of the nation as the central problematic of our time. He also suggests that the question of the nation has to be posed in the context of the intellectual history of nineteenth-century India, and *not* in the context of the history of modern Europe. Aijaz Ahmad makes a similar argument that "The *historically* adequate referent for Indian nationhood exists in India in the shape of the history of the national movement itself" (1997 278; emphasis in the original). Ahmad argues that the political concepts and practices of Western origin such as "nationhood", "constitutionality", "citizenship", "democracy" and "socialism" can no longer be treated as a mere legacy of imperialism; "*Words* may have originated in Europe, but the historical adequacy of the *referent* can only be estalished through reference to practices undertaken within India by Indian political subjects" (1997 279; emphasis in the original).

One of the major political achievements of the modern Indian state, according to Ahmad, is that it became a secular, democratic republic immediately after Independence. But there is an urgency to re-evaluate the political "achievements" of postcolonial India at this time when there is a tendency to take its secular-democratic character for granted. Some of the achievements of this state are the offer of adult franchise to all men and women at the very founding moment of electoral democracy. One can consider these events as the logical consequence of the success of the freedom struggle. But it would only establish an unproblematic continuity between the years that preceded Independence and the years that followed. It is worth noting here that until 1946 franchise was extended to only a small minority of the population and that the nationalists had accepted the prescription of wealth and education as conditions for the exercise of public authority. The extension of franchise to all citizens irrespective of wealth and education is certainly an achievement of the modern Indian state, but it is precisely the one which effectively erased a powerful history of struggle over education and other resources of the country. The politically charged and highly heterogenous articulations of the period preceding Independence were at once rewritten into the quietist languages of social policy and legislative reform. However, the burden of that unresolved struggle continues to inform the various agendas of the Indian state and its education policy as evidenced in the resolutions made in the UGC document. It is also clear that the government resolutions are strategic and they are always haunted by that which they write out of their schemes, plans and proposals. It is important, therefore, to understand the concepts of "nation" and "nationhood" as historically constituted in which education figures as a major site of contestation.

The colonial education system had produced effects that became increasingly contentious during the time of Independence. It was mostly on account of its entanglement with questions of nation, subject and citizenship that the issue of education came to acquire a new dimension. Although the colonial state had made an offer of education to natives it was not its agenda to institute citizenship through education. It had no doubt invented a repertoire of address whereby a native population could be called "the natural-born subjects of Her Majesty". The question of subject and citizenship become more pronounced during the anti-colonial struggle but it acquired a new meaning and a new charge when contestations over citizenship were made within the native community. For example, the struggle over education during the nineteenth and early twentieth century was as much against the colonial state as it was within the native society. While the elite narratives of struggle over education gave primacy to the English/vernacular debate, the struggle within the native society was against the continuing hold of a certain caste/class/community over the resources of education. It is in this context that I propose a reading of B.R. Ambedkar. The significance of Ambedkar lies in his forceful articulation of the relationship between caste and education. He has written so extensively on this particular issue that it makes no sense to try to present here anything like a fair assessment of the richness and complexity of his thought. All I propose to do here is to concentrate on some of his essays in order to show how certain crucial issues relating to access to education are neglected on account of an overemphasis on the English/vernacular debate in mainstream nationalism.[8]

In 1928 Ambedkar submitted to the Indian Statutory Commission a statement concerning the state of education of the Depressed Classes in Bombay Presidency. On the surface, the statement constitutes a sweeping overview of the history of the education policy of the Government from 1813 to 1923. But the significance of the statement lies in its analysis of the history of delegitimization of a certain community through a systematic appraisal of events, years and documents. It is also important to note here that this community of people did not have any fixed designation. Earlier, such designations as "Low castes", "Backward Hindus", "Backward classes", "Depressed Classes", "Untouchables" were used interchangeably; Ambedkar accepts the interchangeability of these descriptions. In fact, it was only with the Government of India Act of 1935 that a semantic stability was forced on what was earlier a community of fluid boundaries. All these designations take the generic title of "Scheduled Castes" with the coming of the 1935 Act. Ambedkar's "State of Education" report, I argue, charts quite effectively the process through which caste emerges as a category of political contestation under the British rule.

Ambedkar begins with a reference to the state of education under the Peshwas. He argues that under the Peshwa government the Depressed Classes were entirely out of the pale of education. What was the reason for such a deprivation? Ambedkar's answer is: "for the simple reason that the Peshwa's Government was a theocracy based upon the canons of Manu, according to which the Shudras and Atishudras [classes corresponding to the Backward Classes of the Education department], if they had any right to life, liberty and property had certainly no right to education" (1928 409). The advent of the British rule, according to Ambedkar, raised hopes among the Depressed Classes as they thought that the British administra-tion promised a democracy "which believed in the principle of one man, one value, be that man high or low" (1928 409). The point of comparison however ends there as Ambedkar goes on to show how "the British Government deliberately ruled that education was to be a preserve for the higher classes" (1928 409). He shows how it was argued in the Report of the Board of Education of the Bombay Presidency for the Year 1850-51 that "Educational Boards ought not to allow themselves to be distracted from a more limited practical field of action by the visionary speculations of uninformed benevolence" (in Ambedkar 1928 412). The question, therefore, was not merely of whether to give education through English or the vernaculars, but, more importantly, of how to ascertain "the field of action", which would be "practical" and not "visionary". To put it differently, the difficulty with the Government was how to fix the precise extent of the native population to which education should penetrate.

Ambedkar refers to the particular difficulty which the colonial state had to face in deciding what "upper classes" exactly meant in the context of India. He refers to the kind of injunctions that were often made to the European inquirer "to divert his mind of European analogies which so often insinuated themselves almost involuntarily into Anglo-Indian speculations" (in Ambedkar 1928 413). Ambedkar points out that the colonial government believed that in England there was a clear line which separated the upper classes from the lower classes in terms of manners, wealth, political and social influence, but no such line of separation obtained in the colonial society. Hence, the government had to put together such a class. What, therefore, came to be desigated as "upper classes" consisted of the following people in the native society:

1st. The land owners and jaghirdars, representatives of the former feudatories and persons in authorities under Native Powers, and who may be termed the Soldier class.

2nd. Those who have acquired wealth in trade or commerce or the commercial class.

3rd. The higher *employees* of Government.

4th. Brahmins with whom may be associated though at long interval those of higher castes of writers who live by the pen such as Prabhus and Shenvis in Bombay, Kayasthas in Bengal, provided they acquire a position either in learning or station. (in Ambedkar 1928 413; emphasis in the original).

Ambedkar, however, goes on to show how the British official opinion before 1855 was decidedly in favour of the brahmins. The official analysis demonstrated that "the influential class whom the Government are able to avail themselves of in diffusing the seeds of education are the Brahmins and other high castes *Brahmannis proximi*" (in Ambedkar 1928 412). Ambedkar notes that in the Despatch of 1854 the Court of Directors recognized the neglect on the part of the government to educate "the great mass of the people who are utterly incapable of obtaining any education worthy of the name by their own efforts" (1928 415). However, he refers to the Hunter Commission of 1882 to show that "although mass education was the policy of the government, the masses were as outside the pale of education as they were before the year 1854 and that the lowest and aboriginal classes of the Hindus still remained lowest in order of education; so much so that in 1881-82 there was no student from that community either in the High Schools or in the colleges of the presidency" (1928 417). The lifting of the ban on the education of the Depressed Classes, Ambedkar argued, was a nominal affair as "the ban continued in practice as before" (1928 419). In order to show how the principle of non-exclusion was in fact compromised in practical operation. Ambekar gives the example of a petition submitted to the government in June 1856 by a Mahar boy who had complained that "though willing to pay the usual schooling fee, he had been denied admission to the Dharwar Government School". (in Ambedkar 1928 418) The Government Resolution of July 1856 admitted that "the Mahar petitioner has abstract justice on his side" and that "the disadvantage under which the petitioner labours is not one which has originated with this government". But the resolution held that the "Government is obliged to keep in mind that to interfere with the prejudices of ages in a summary manner, for the sake of one or a few individuals, would probably do a great damage to the cause of education" (in Ambedkar 1928 418).

The government in its effort to find a way out of the "impasse" created by the "prejudices of ages", says Ambedkar, adopted two measures: (1) the institution of separate government schools for low-caste boys; and, (2) the extension of special encouragement to missionary bodies to undertake their education by relaxing the rules in grant-in-aid. However, the opening of separate schools was given up in practice as it involved expenses unacceptable "to a Government to which primary education was a task" (1928 424). Besides, the provision that such schools should be opened where Backward Classes were in large number, according to Ambedkar, worked against the Backward Classes as they could "seldom be found to be living in one locality in large numbers" (1928 424). The stocktaking by the Hunter Commission in 1882 showed only a very meagre presence of Backward Classes in primary education and no presence at all in the secondary and college education. Ambedkar further cites the Report of the Director of Public Instruction, Bombay Presidency for the year 1923-24 which showed "no improvement over the situation as it stood in 1882 relatively speaking" (1928 421). In the matter of population, the Backward Classes were greater in number but in the matter of education they occupied a place which was not only last but the least. The "Advanced Hindus", on the other hand, occupied the fourth place in order of population but they were first in order of college education, first in order of secondary education and first in order of primary education. This according to Ambedkar, reveals "the disparity that exists in the educational advancement of the different communities" (1928 421).

Ambedkar's "State of Education" report of 1928 can be better understood in relation to the historical development of elite nationalist politics in India. To the mainstream nationalists of the pre-Independence period, the "main enemy" in India was imperialism. Ambedkar, no doubt, agreed that the Backward Classes needed national independence to have a stake in political power. But for him the internal caste/class exploiter was no less an enemy. He, in fact, declared that it hardly mattered whether the exploiter was a Hindu or a European: "The Hindu is as alien to him [the untouchable] as a European is" (1945 425). For him both imperialism and feudalism/casteism are indissolubly connected. In his speech at the Round Table Conference in 1930 he declared:

> That the British, who have held so large a sway over us for such a long time, have done some good we cheerfully acknowledge. But, there is certainly no fundamental change in our position. Indeed, so far as we were concerned, the British Government has accepted the social arrangements as it found them, and has preserved them faithfully in the manner of the Chinese tailor who, when given an old coat as a pattern, produced with pride an exact replica, rents, patches and all. Our wrongs have remained as open sores and they have not been righted, although 150 years of British rule have rolled away (1930 504).

The British Government, according to Ambedkar, neither intended nor was equipped to bring about any revolutionary change in the social politics of India. It suffered from two serious limitations: "There is first an internal limitation which arises from the character, motives and interests of those who are in power...The second consideration that limits its authority is the mortal fear it has of external resistance" (1930 505). Within these limits, however, the British Government affected certain changes serious enough to transform the traditional forms of dominance and resistance into modern forms. By transforming the dominant castes into a unified bureaucracy the British Government established a link between social dominance and state power. Ambedkar's argument that the hundred and fifty years of British rule produced only "an exact replica" of traditional social arrangements was not meant to emphasize the changelessness in the native society. Rather, it was intended to show how the British rule only strengthened the traditional social structure and empowered the already powerful.

Ambedkar argued that the changes brought about by the British hardly had any effect on the native social structure in spite of the "modern" conditions created by the colonial state where "men of all castes and races work side by side in the mill without any misgiving regarding the caste of their neighbours" (1932 493). Ambedkar's observation had reference to the popular perception that this co-mingling of caste under modern conditions was evidence of the disappearance of the caste system. But Ambedkar argued that the everyday life in the colonial society had made it impossible for the upper castes to follow the same rules they had followed a hundred years ago. The educated upper castes who were aspiring for ranks in the colonial society had effectively adjusted to the demands of modernity. They had come to deny caste in public spaces while practising it privately. This, according to Ambedkar, was a "modern" phenomenon of caste peculiar to society under the colonial rule. He cites the statement made by the Census Superintendent of Bihar and Orissa in 1921 that the non-observance of caste in native society need not be regarded as a "sign portending the collapse of the caste system, but of its adjustment to modern conditions" (1932 493).

It was precisely in the context of such "modern" practices of the caste system that Ambedkar was critical of the "reforms" introduced by the upper-caste/upper-class intelligensia. Ambedkar argued that "while the intelligentsia is a very important part of Indian society, it is drawn from its upper strata and although it speaks in the name of the country and leads the political movement, it has not shed the narrow particularism of the class from which it is drawn" (1930 506). It was often argued by the nationalist intelligentsia that "the problem of the Depressed Classes is a social problem and that its solution lies elsewhere than in politics" (1930 506). The Congress-led political movement, according to Ambedkar, consistently avoided the issue of social reform on the pretext that "we stand upon a common platform—here we have all agreed to bury our social, religious differences and recognize one common fact that being subjects of the same Soverign and living under the same Government and the same political institutions, we have common rights and common grievances" (in Ambedkar 1945 10). This statment by Surendranath Bannerjee, the Congress President in 1895, echoed the words of W.C. Bannerjee who in his presidential address in 1892 had declared: "I am one of those who have very little faith in the public discussion of social matters; those are things which I think, ought to be left to the individuals of a community who belong to the same social organization to do what they can do for its improvement... the Congress commenced and has since remained, and will, I sincerely trust, always remain as purely political organization devoting its energies to political matters and political matters only" (in Ambedkar 1945 9). In his reading of the history of Congress party, Ambedkar showed how efforts were made by the Congress intelligensia to keep the social issue separate from the political and how the representatives of the Depressed Classes were against such a separation. In 1917 a resolution was made in a public meeting of the Depressed Classes which maintained that the disabilities imposed by religion and custom worked against their admission into public schools, hospitals, courts of justice and public offices. It also resolved that "these disabilities, social in origin, amount in law and practice to political disabilities and as such fall legitimately within the political mission and propaganda of the Indian National Congress" (in Ambedkar 1945 15).

The struggle over the social and the political was at the heart of the debate during India's struggle over freedom. The Congress, according to Ambedkar, regarded the freedom of India from the British imperialism to be the be-all and end-all of Indian nationalism. Against this view Ambedkar held that there were two different aspects to the politics of India which he called "foreign politics" and "constitutional politics". India's foreign politics "relates to India's freedom from British Imperialism, while the constitutional politics of India centres round the nature of a constitution for a free India" (1945 440). However, the constitutional demands made by the Depressed Classes for safeguards and guarantees for minimum representation in the legislature, executive and public services were held by the Congress as expressions not only of "communalism" but also of "pro-British" attitudes and the leaders of the Depressed Classes were also called "job-hunters" (Ambedkar 1945 170). The Congress leadership maintained that:

> What the Indians must aim at is to maintain in India an efficient body politic and that this can be done only by insisting that every place of power and authority should be filled by none but the best men available (in Ambedkar 1945 474).

The Congress attitude to the Depressed Class demand for reservation in public services only consolidated the attitude of the brahmins and the allied castes who had argued that "efficiency" should be "the only consideration in the matters of appointment to public services and that caste and creed should count for nothing" (1929 394). The brahminical notion of efficiency was based on educational merit and the Congress leadership invoked it to justify appointment by open competition as against by reservation. The argument for open competition has no doubt an "appearance of fairness" but, according to Ambedkar, it "completely fails to carry conviction when in practice one finds that having regard to the historical circumstances of India every time the 'best man' is chosen, he turns out to be a man from the governing class" (1945 475)—the class which still consists principally of brahmins and allied castes.

Through a careful examination of the role of caste in the promotion of education in the colonial society Ambedkar showed how the supremacy of the brahmin was neither a matter of historical accident nor of superior intellect—"for intellect is nobody's monopoly" (1945 477)—but was enmeshed with the question of domination, exploitation and oppression. Ambedkar's intervention provides a rethinking of the question of merit and efficiency. The uncritical acceptance of the educational merit of a particular caste/class/community had and continues to have enormous effect on the conduct of Indian politics. Ambedkar's "State of Education" report shows that education, which was a major site of contestation in the colonial society, eventually promoted the advancement of "the upper classes". The question of caste was crucial to the question of self-government which involved issues of franchise, representation and electoral power. In the Round Table Conference Speech in 1930, Ambedkar had specially criticized the proposal for a franchise based on literacy by saying that "literacy in India is so unevenly distributed, that some communities would have all the increase of the franchise added to their stock, while other communities would remain where they are" (1930a 562).

The introduction of adult franchise at the dawn of the Indian independence, however, seems to have severed the link between caste and education. But a reading of Ambedkar in independent India, I believe, is useful for understanding the return of the caste question. The Mandal Commission Report reiterated the complicity of caste and education. By raising the issue of "reservations" in the services, it brought in the question of merit and efficiency back into the political discourse of our time. This reading of Ambedkar suggests that the idea of education as a site where "merit" and "efficiency" are produced is problematic. In fact, his understanding of education in terms of the political and the social opens up the question of merit itself.

What is equally significant is that Ambedkar's writings are hardly concerned with the English-vernacular question. The issue in his writings relates to the question of differential access to education and the modernization of caste. The question of the democratization of education through the vernacular thus becomes problematic in the face of evidence showing a systematic denial of education to the "Depressed Classes". Caste critiques of education keep our focus on the production of privilege in the social and political domain, often through incisive analysis of the notions of merit and efficiency produced through education, whereas the elite debates over education centre around the assumed opposition between the colonial and the indigenous. This opposition often manifested in the form of an English–vernacular divide. In the following chapter, I will examine the national elite's manner of engagement with the vernacular question focussing on its implications for national education.

NOTES

1. See, for example, C.A. Bayly, *The New Cambridge History of India: Indian Society and the Making of the British Empire*. Cambridge: Cambridge UP, 1988, (x).
2. *Subaltern Studies,* in many ways, represents a significant movement in Indian historiography. The work of Subaltern writers is substantial and often related to each other only loosely. Hence, instead of a futile attempt at a summary, I have focussed on those essays which theorize the Subaltern project; primarily Ranajit Guha, "On Some Aspects of the Historiography of Colonial India," *Subaltern Studies I* (New Delhi: Oxford UP, 1982) 1-7, Dipesh Chakrabarty, "An Invitation to a Dialogue," *Subaltern Studies IV* (New Delhi: Oxford UP, 1985) 364–376 and Guha, "Dominance Without Hegemony and Its Historiography," *Subaltern Studies VI* (New Delhi: Oxford UP, 1989) 210–309.
3. Partha Chatterjee has also made this point in *Nationalist Thought and the Colonial World: A Derivative Discourse?* (New Delhi: Oxford UP, 1986). See 36–53.
4. For a detailed exposition of the Subaltern project, see Chakrabarty, 1985, 364–376.
5. See, for example, David Hardiman, *Peasant Nationalists of Gujarat: Kheda District, 1917-1934* (New Delhi: Oxford UP, 1981) and Shahid Amin, *Event, Metaphor, Memory: Chauri Chaura, 1922-1992* (New Delhi: Oxford UP, 1995).
6. *Guidelines to the Universities for Preparation of Development Proposals for the Seventh Plan*, University Grants Commission, New Delhi, 1986.
7. See, for example, Dipesh Chakrabarty, "Postcoloniality and the Artifice of History: Who Speaks for 'Indian' Pasts?" in *A Subaltern Studies Reader 1986-1995*, ed., Ranajit Guha (New Delhi: Oxford UP, 1998) 263–293; Vivek Dhareshwar, "'Our Time': History, Sovereignty and Politics" *Economic and Political Weekly* 30.6 (1995): 317–324; Sudipta Kaviraj, "The Imaginary Institution of India," *Subaltern Studies VII*, eds. Partha Chatterjee and Gyanendra Pandey (New Delhi: Oxford UP, 1992) 1–39. Partha Chatterjee, *The Nation and Its Fragments* (New Delhi: Oxford UP, 1994).
8. The two texts that I have referred to extensively are "Statement Concerning the State of Education of the Depressed Classes in the Bombay Presidency," (1928) *Writings and Speeches*, Vol. 2. (Bombay: Education Department, Government of Maharashtra, 1982) 407–428 and *What Congress and Gandhi Have Done to the Untouchables*, 1945, Vol. 9 of *Writings and Speeches* (Bombay: Education Department, Government of Maharashtra, 1991). For all other citations, refer *Bibliography*.

Three

English and the Politics of the Vernacular

SECTION I
ON POSING THE QUESTION OF THE VERNACULAR

In the previous chapter, I suggested that colonial-national struggles often translated into the English-vernacular debate. In this chapter I will focus on the manner in which the vernacular was shaped through nationalism. I will argue that the national elite invoked the vernacular as a counter to the imposition of an "alien" language. However, the reshaping of the vernacular for nation and modernity constructed it in terms closely linked to the nature and function of English. In tracking the emergence of the modern vernacular in the demands for a vernacular university (first section), the fashioning of national education (second section) and the nativization of the lyric form in Gujarati (third section), my attempt will be to show that the relationship between English and the vernacular is more collaborative than oppositional. In the last section, I will argue that despite national characterization of the vernacular as popular, the vernacular in its present form is as alienating as English.

In 1870 the Vice Chancellor of Calcutta University, Edward C. Bayley declared: "I would disclaim all sympathy with the 'Orientalism', which was overthrown and deservedly overthrown, some five and thirty years ago" (1870 101). Bayley was clearly referring to Lord Macaulay's Minute of 1835 which was supposed to have "overthrown" Orientalism and to have inaugurated the phase of Anglicism in colonial education policy. The occasion for Bayley's declaration was the proposal made for the creation of a vernacular university in the North Western Provinces. A historically situated reading of the vernacular debate over education, particularly in the context of the demand for a vernacular university, could allow us to put into perspective certain commonly held assumptions about "Orientalism" and its relationship with the vernacular.

In 1867 the British Indian Association of North Western Provinces submitted a petition to the Viceroy and Governor General of India in Council pleading for the use of modern Indian languages to impart "European knowledge". Earlier to 1837 education in the schools was given through the vernacular; however, the demand for the vernacular in higher education served not only as a comment on the existing system of higher education but also inaugurated a fresh debate over some of the provisions made in the Education Despatch of 1854.

The Despatch of 1854 had made a distinction between the vernacular language as a medium of instruction and English language as an essential requisite for higher education. Consequently, the entire system of education with its hierarchy of schools and colleges reflected the asymmetrical relationship of languages. However, such an arrangement with English for higher education and the vernacular for popular education was not intended to be permanent. It was envisaged in the Despatch that "as the importance of the vernacular languages becomes more appreciated, the vernacular literature of India will be gradually enriched by translations of European books, or by the original compositions of men whose minds have been imbued with the spirit of European advancement, so that European knowledge may gradually be placed in this manner within the reach of all classes of people" (Oliphant et al 368).

Commentaries on the Orientalist and Anglicist debate have always gone back to Wood's Despatch of 1854 to show the aggressive side of the Anglicist position. It is true that English was recommended as the language of instruction but it was clearly stated that it was neither the "aim nor desire to substitute the English language for the vernacular dialects of the country" (Oliphant et al. 367). In fact, it was broadly agreed that any efficient system of education would necessarily have to replace English with the vernacular.

It was precisely in the context of such a provision for the venacular that a demand was made in 1867 to impart higher education through the instrumentality of the vernacular. It was argued that "an examination in the vernacular be annually held in those very subjects, in which the student is now examined in English in the Calcutta University, and that degrees now confered on English students for proficiency in various departments of knowledge, be likewise conferred on the students who successfully pass in the same subjects in the vernacular" (Mookerjee et al. 27). The demand for a university degree in the vernacular subjects might look natural in independent India, but such a demand in 1867 meant that the degrees offered in English subjects be made equivalent to the ones offered in the vernacular examinations.

Calcutta University was founded on the assumption that "true knowledge, in its higher branches, can only be imparted to the people of India through the English language, and that the only literature that has any value is that of Europe" (Bayley 1868 41). Such an assumption came under stress when a similar status was claimed for the vernacular. In fact, the colonial government pointed out promptly that any attempt to establish equivalence between an English and vernacular degree would "materially degrade the character and lessen the value of an Indian University degree" (Bayley 1869 56). The petition submitted by the British Indian Association, however, had only pleaded for the possible arrangement of an alliance: "The system we propose may be different from that now in vogue, but it is not antagonistic to it, the ultimate object of both is the same. What we urge is that instead of English alone, the vernacular also may be made the channel for the instruction of all the people alike in the very highest subjects of culture and education" (Mookerjee et al. 25).

The colonial government was committed to the cause of the vernacular in principle but the demand for its application meant the creation of a vernacular university. What was perceived to be at stake was the imperial character of the university education in India. The Universities of Calcutta, Bombay and Madras, it was argued, were at least "founded on the same general principle" (Bayley 1877 222), even though doubts were expressed about the comparative worth of the degrees offered at Bombay and Madras. But the proposed vernacular university repudiated those educational principles by insisting on an education through the vernacular. E.C. Bayley, who was quick to see in the move for a vernacular university the emergence of a certain "Orientalism", warned the colonial government in 1877 of the dangers in "reversing the policy of centralizing university influence" (Bayley 1877 219) under the influence of local demands.

The terms in which the debate over Orientalism was set up in the 1860s and 1870s were certainly based on a new agenda. The earlier agenda was "to make the classical languages of the East the media for European knowledge" (Bayley 1870 101), but the new demand was not merely for a "pure Oriental learning of the old type" (Thibaut 407). The British Indian Association had made it clear in its petition that "by the terms, education through the vernacular, we do not mean the revival of Asiatic learning and science as subjects of instruction. On the contrary, we seek only the diffusion of sciences and arts now prevalent in Europe, since we aim at nothing else than the universal spread of European Enlightenment throughout India" (Mookerjee et al. 25). The petitioners, while acknowledging the benefits of education through the English language, observed that these benefits were confined to only a small section of the natives. They further argued that the achievements of "these few are insignificant when compared with the great majority, and this majority has received no enlightenment and in fact has not been affected at all" (23). The spread of education, it was felt, would be limited if instruction is imparted through a language "which is foreign and unknown and can never be acquired by the vast majority of the 140 millions of British India" (25).

The argument in favour of vernacular education, however, was never made in opposition to an education in English.

Instead, it drew its strength from an implied conviction that the vernacular can be a possible ally of English. The petitioners argued that education through the vernacular would benefit "not the few only but the large masses of the people" (Mookerjee et al. 23). In 1869 Sir D. Macleod, Lieutenant-Governor of the Punjab expressed doubts over the efficacy of Macaulay's filtration theory by saying that "the great majority of those most highly trained by us have, by that training, been rendered almost as alien to the bulk of their countryman, as we are ourselves" (53).

Macleod's observation was in tune with the arguments of the petitioners. He had argued that in spite of the success of English education in promoting intellectual development of students, its "exotic" character did not allow it "as a means of raising a nation into robust and healthy activity, permeating the mass and bringing all classes into suitable relations with each other" (52). He thought that the task of "raising a nation" and "permeating the mass" could be better accomplished by the vernacular languages as instruments of education. English education had declined into mere "rote-learning" and "word-acquiring" (Kempson 84) and therefore needed to be substituted by the vernacular. But Kempson redefined vernacular education in terms of its interlacing with "an Occidental, rather than an Oriental form" (84). He suggests that the spoken tongues would lay "the foundations of a future and more self-expansive enlightenment" (84), an idea that launched the trajectory of vernacular education in tandem with the English. The proposed vernacular university was envisaged not merely to offer education through the vernacular medium, but to help raise "men thoroughly competent to re-produce in an Oriental garb the morality [Moral and Mental Philosophy] and science of Europe and to raise the dignity of the vernacular with the aid of its cognate classical language" (Reid 79). As M.S. Howell argued, this university would help in the development of native thinkers and writers who "when their scholastic and university career is terminated... may be put into a position to increase more effectually by their own writings the diffusion of knowledge amongst their countrymen" (70).

However, the relationship between the demand for a vernacular university and the desire for the development of the vernacular literature was somewhat problematic. The argument that a shift from English to the vernacular would produce creative works of merit did not seem to have a strong basis. The example of Bengali literature was cited to demonstrate that "it was precisely those who distinguished themselves by their mastery of the English tongue... devoted themselves to the formation of a healthy literature in their own language" (Bose 310-11). Bayley wrote in 1870 that "the last thirty years, during which it [Bangalee language] is said to have been enriching itself so largely from Sanskrit sources, has been precisely the period in which enormous efforts have been made at great expense and with remarkable success to spread English Education in Lower Bengal" (1870 104). Bayley was suggesting that English education did not necessarily work against the interests of either the vernacular or of Sanskrit. The improvement, enrichment and expansion of the vernacular, according to Bayley, should be guided by "natural laws" and should not be controlled "artifically" by the endeavours of Government (1870 104). A.M. Bose, Secretary of the Indian Association in Calcutta made a similar argument by saying that "foreigners, however learned and well-intentioned, can never hope to form the literature of another people and the only way in which they can help in the formation of such a literature is by bestowing on the people a *sound education* and thus enabling them to create a literature for themselves" (310, emphasis added).

Both the Orientalists and Anglicists emphasized the improvement of the vernaculars. In fact, the new Orientalism of the 1860s and 1870s marked a crucial phase in the history of education in India as it tried to rework Orientalism within the premises of Anglicism. Such a reworking needed a rearrangement of the existing system of education. Although the Orientalists and Anglicists had different views on the question of language to be used in educational institutions, both had faith in the capacity of these institutions to improve and develop the vernacular languages. Both considered English and the vernaculars as potential allies in the spread of the ideas of the European enlightenment and civilization among the natives. In their demand for a vernacular university the British Indian Association had only set the terms for a possible alliance between these two seemingly opposite groups: "while maintaining and promoting English education, can we not adopt a verncular lanugage, as a medium better suited than a strange tongue for the general diffusion of knowledge and the general reform of ideas, manners and morals of the people?" (Mookerjee et al. 25).

The new Orientalism had also brought the question of the vernacular to a state of crisis. M.S. Howell acknowledged that "Hindustani boys should be taught, like English boys, in their own vernacular, because that mode is more expeditious and more sure" (70) and "more within the comprehension of the people" (67). But questions were legitimately raised as to which language was exactly meant to be "vernacular". In the context of the North Western Provinces it was held that there are not one but two vernaculars—Urdu and Hindi. This pushed M.S. Howell to address the problem of the "educational vernacular" by arguing that "the development of two rival vernaculars within comparatively so small a tract of country as the North-Western provinces would be fatal to national intellectual progress" (73). In fact, the issue of the educational vernacular in 1868 marked the beginning of a difficulty in the education system which had to cater to the diverse linguistic heritage of people living in an administrative unit called the "province". This difficulty continued to influence subsequent thinking on the subject and finally occupied the centre-stage during the linguistic creation of states in independent India. The issue of the vernacular, therefore, has a clear political dimension. Bayley had, in fact, argued that the demand for a vernacular university was "not educational, but political", evinced in a certain class of people "who have not acquired and are not likely to any great extent acquire, English" (1870a 101). According to him, ambitions of these people were "stimulated" by watching the the progress made by people in other provinces through English. The recognition of the educational as the political problematizes any easy association between the demand for a vernacular education and the claim for democratization of education. There is clearly a need to reiterate the political dimension of the vernacular which remains under erasure on account of the way it has been constituted in the literary-aesthetic domain.

The terms around which the debate over the vernacular was conducted however suggests that the issue was sought to be resolved at the realm of pedagogy with little, or no attention to its political aspect. It was argued that the issue belonged to the domain of pedagogy: "if teaching be not in the language in which the pupil thinks, and illustration by objects and associations with which he is conversant, intellectual development becomes dwarfed and stunted" (Elliott 118). The focus on the pedagogical aspect of the vernacular pushed the political aspect out of the domain of engagement and reduced the issue to the task of producing a "suitable" language and literature for the purpose of teaching. "The great want of the people is a vernacular literature;—works in History, Art and Science, containing sound knowledge, written in an elegant style, and composed on models of thought and expression agreeable to the native mind" (Simson 1869 93). Although the demand for a vernacular university could be seen as a demand to democratize the sphere of education and to challenge the supremacy of English, it would be more productive to see in this demand the rise of a certain provincialism spearheaded by the vernacular elite of a certain class/caste background. However, such a rearrangement of education along the lines of the vernacular with a corresponding rearrangement in aesthetics and pedagogy, produced, as recent studies have shown, an enormous effect on the native perception of language and literature. In the subsequent sections I will explore the complex negotiations that were underway between English education and the fashioning of vernacular languages and literature in India.

SECTION II
SISTER NIVEDITA ON NATIONAL EDUCATION

The focus in this section would be on Sister Nivedita's papers on national education in India.[1] A close look at these papers would reveal how a quasi-religious national identity is shaped by a careful writing of the language of religion into a discourse of the nation. It would also show how her proposal for a Sanskritized vernacular education is problematic in the face of diversity of language and religion in India. In fact, Sister Nivedita's mission can be read as an attempt to write "an Upanishad of the National History [that] would make eternal foundation for the Indian Nationality in the Indian heart, the only world in which the nationality can be built enduringly" (104). One could see how such a history is produced by a systematic placing of the liberal, humanist ideas of the west alongside the "civilizational" values of the Indian past. In the process, India is mapped onto a Western framework of national development. A clear example of such a mapping can be gleaned through the following passage:

> Henceforth they [the Indian People] will understand—indeed they have understood for several years past—that even schooling has to justify itself to the conscience of the schooled by the great law of sacrifice and that this law here is the development of the child for the good, not of himself, but of *Jana Desh-Dharma* or, as the Western would phrase it, the development of the individual for the benefit of the environment. (27)

One can see here the insertion of a Western vocabulary into the political imaginary of the native. Here, the development of the individual for the benefit of the environment is made to stand for the development of the child for the good of *Jana-Desh-Dharma.* Of course, such a translation of the Western into the Indian is fraught with the realization that the Western vocabulary is the product of a particular conjuncture in Western history and that the vocabulary which is supposedly Indian is of a Sanskritized and brahminic variety. However, this uncomfortable realization is overcome, in the above passage, through a systematic suppression of the respective histories of these two sets of vocabularies. In fact, their easy translation in the passage is an indication that the Western political vocabulary is complicitous with the Sanskritized Indian vocabulary in producing the nation and its history. But, as we see and as Nivedita would argue, it is education which would naturalize the politics of such a translation, making the rite of passage look natural and normal.

Nivedita's course in national education is designed to ensure the smooth movement of Western language and thought into the Indian as that would constitute India's entry into the modern world, into knowledge itself. "Knowledge is one", Nivedita says. "In pure knowledge and therefore, in science, there can be neither native nor foreign" (42). And it is this knowledge which is to form a part of her agenda for national education in India.

She perceives for India "the task of conveying modern knowledge in the tongues of women and the people" (63). "How are people to understand Indian history" she asks, "if they have first to learn a foreign language?" (63). She knew that the spread of modern, Western forms of knowledge through a foreign tongue would be slow and very limited in scope. One way to expedite the process would be to make that knowledge form available in the vernaculars. The development of the vernaculars, she believed, would not only end the hegemony of Sanskrit but would guarantee the speedy availability of the modern spirit to people at large. She also argued that since Sanskrit was considered the repository of traditional knowledge in India an apology for the dissemination of that knowledge in the vernaculars would seem normal. Nivedita argues that the task of conserving tradition and culture need not lie in the hands of the antiquarian or the pedant; it should be made available to people in general.

Nivedita, therefore, proposes a thorough democratization of traditional Indian forms of knowledge which are available only in Sanskrit to be disseminated through the vernaculars. Such a process, she argued, would lead to the production of a set of Sanskritized vernaculars which would then release culture from the hegemony of the Sanskrit language and its scholars. Although in her proposal there is an assumption that the entry of culture into the vernacular would end the hegemony of the Sanskrit language and literature, what her proposal does not take into account is the new form of hegemony which the Sanskritized vernaculars would come to exercise on native cultures. She seems to be occupied more in setting up a possible vernacular study of cultures, with its energy drawn from both native and foreign souces. This could be one of the reasons why she associates the process of vernacularization with democratization of cultures and, by extension, democratization of studies on culture. Nivedita, therefore, goes on to argue that "the form may be foreign; but the life, the energy, the holiness of dedication will be Indian and know themselves for Indian. The whole body of knowledge can be assimilated easily by the native who is rooted and grounded in his relation to his own country" (50).

The anxiety of a foreign influence which haunts through Nivedita's writing is temporarily resolved through the recognition that cultural forms "are some old, some new, but the ideal itself knows nothing of time" (50). She argues that a national education should release our imagination which is made up of familiar and known elements of our cultural past. It should lead us through the limiting forms of our and other people's culture which are time and space specific. It should lead us to the ideal and "when we reach the ideal itself, we have reached the eternal. Here all humanity is at one. Here there is neither new, nor old, neither own nor foreign" (35).

The logical fallout of such an assertion is that there is an ideal form of knowledge which can be realized by all people at all places and at all times. This also would mean that the real test of our education would lie in the degree to which we have attained to this ideal, this universal. "This is the necessary condition," Nivedita writes, "of all healthy education in all countries whatever their political position or stage of development" (29).

Nivedita, thus, resolves the question of cultural difference by proposing a democratized form of education where the vernacular is requisitioned for the dissipation of anxiety concerning cultural invasion from the West with both Sanskrit and English playing secondary role to the vernacular. "The true differentiae of the Hindu mind" Nivedita says, "is not a preoccupation with Sanskrit" (101). Thus, by defining Hindu identity away from Sanskrit, Nivedita reclaims the position of the vernacularists, carefully co-opting them as partners in the nation-building project. But the proposed identity, in the context of nation-making, as we would see, is problematic in many ways. On one hand, it produces a hegemony of the vernacular, quite in the manner of Sanskrit. The form of the vernacular which shapes itself in the model of the Sanskrit delegitimizes other forms of the vernacular. On the other hand, by mapping the national and the modern in India across the Sanskrit-vernacular axis, Nivedita's proposal keeps the vernacular out of the reach of a whole lot of people, for example, the dalits, tribals, leave aside the minorities. Neverthless, Nivedita finds a space for these marginalized groups in her national project by proposing a shared identity, which she thinks can be realized by emulating the spirit of a modern Indian who is given to the course of humanity, of people, of country and who is free from the limits of the local. "There is a level of achievement," Nivedita writes in a self-assured tone, "where all educated persons of the world can meet, understand and enjoy each other's associations. This level is freedom. Intellectually speaking, it is *Mukti*" (39). In fact, she argues that national education in India should ensure the production of "an oriental in whom orientalism had been intensified, while to it had been added the Western conception of the cause of Humanity, of the Country, of the People as a whole, Western power of initiative and organisation, Western energy and Practicality—such an ideal should inspire our energy of culture in the East" (69).

Here, in Nivedita's language, we see the outlines of a problem relating to the question of identity on the one hand and the question of language on the other. There is no doubt that the language question in India is tied to the formation of the vernacular literature in India. There is no wonder that literature in contemporary India has emerged as a site where contestations over identity are made and the political aspect of language is returned to the domain of the literary and the aesthetic as one of its constituent element. In the following section I will the instance of take a vernacular writer and his method of writing to show how the modern vernacular has constituted the literary–aesthetic domain by a systematic disavowal of the political.

SECTION III
NARSINHRAO AND THE REFASHIONING OF VERNACULAR LITERATURE

In this section my concern would be to track the Indian trajectory of Romanticism and its crucial role in the fashioning of a modernized literary vernacular. We know that Romanticism enabled a new kind of poetry-writing in India. In what follows I will trace the development of this new form and its peculiar history in India/Gujarat through an illustrative reading of a late nineteenth-century Gujarati poet-critic Narsinhrao B. Divetia (1856–1937), popularly known as Narsinhrao. He belongs to what is known as the *Pandit Yug* (The Age of Scholars) in the history of Gujarati Literature. Like many of the fellow litterateurs of his generation, he was educated in English and one of his ambitions was to acquaint his Gujarati readers with some of the finest tenets of Romantic poetry. Literary historians like Umashankar Joshi and others have remarked how Narsinhrao's nature poetry combined the emotional richness of English Romantic poets with the linguitic elegance of Sanskrit and how it was received "ecstatically" by the "Wordsworh and Shelley-loving youth of Gujarat" (356). He is, in fact, hailed as the Wordsworth of Gujarati poetry (Mehd 3-4).[2]

Nature poetry certainly had existed in both Sanskrit and folk traditions in India before the arrival of English Romantic poetry. But the arrival of English Romantic poetry played a crucial role in modernizing vernacular poetry under colonialism. In fact, India's acquaintance with Romanticism is inseparable from the beginnings of English education in India. Through this education and study of English literature, Romanticism as a literary impulse became firmly entrenched in the Indian sensibility during the second half of the nineteenth century. Besides, one knows that English Romantic poetry was enriched by German and French ideas. It is therefore arguable that what came to be studied as English Romantic poetry acquainted English-educated Indians with a wide range of European writers. Infact, the Indian understanding of Romanticism was not confined to the writers of the Romantic Revival in England. It was informed as much by the impact of writers like Shakespeare and Tennyson as by Wordsworth, Coleridge and Keats. For example, Narsinhrao's understanding of Romanticism emerged out of his engagement with writers ranging from Shakespeare, Suckling, Carlyle, Wordsworth, Coleridge and Keats to Tennyson, Max Müller, Goethe, Wagner, Rousseau and Poe.[3] It is a fact that the English education which the vernacular writers acquired under colonialism was largely European in its configuration and was not simply British. In fact, the composition of literary studies in colonial India was quite in tune with the way it was envisaged by Mathew Arnold. We have seen in the first chapter how Arnold's cosmopolitanism was eurocentric and how it was in the service of colonialism. Although English education in the contex of such an "expansive" Arnoldian definition produced a grand idea about literature, one has to take into account the effects that the process of institutionalization had on the production of literature in the colonies. One needs to develop a more nuanced and complex account of our encounter with "English" Literature under colonialism and its effect on creative and critical practice in India. My argument is that an expansive and universalist idea of literature which got institutionalized under colonialism had a precise function. It consolidated the idea that literary values are same everywhere and that these values can be espoused by all, much like literary forms and genres. In my reading of Narsinhrao, I have explored the extent to which he was influenced by such an idea of literature and the extent to which it had shaped his literary and critical practice.

Narsinhrao was the first Gujarati poet who acknowledged freely the influence of Romanticism in his poetry and wrote Romantic poetry in his native language.[4] The issue here is not the success or failure of his poetic enterprise. Many critics have alleged that in his attempts to write Romantic poetry he resembles a schoolboy who masters a particular metre and then incessantly tries to flesh it out with a certain type of subject matter (Mehd 30). If such criticism is taken seriously it is possible to call his poetry "formulaic" (Joshi 363). Sometimes his poetry is described as instances of "fancy" and not "imagination" (Mehd 30). The application of such Coleridgean notions are ways of expressing dissatisfaction with his type of poetry. In fact, the allegation that Narsinhrao's Romanticism stays only at the level of precepts and fails in practice speaks about the expectations of the native critics about what should constitute romantic poetry.[5] Viewed differently, his "formulaic" poetry may yield some interesting insights into the way he nativized Romanticism and fashioned a new form of poetry in Gujarati.

The form of poetry Narsinhrao introduced and popularized in Gujarati was the lyric. His long and laborious essays on the nature of the lyric are evidence of some of his attempts to create a conceptual space for this new form of poetry in the vernacular.[6] In fact, he was engaged in a lively debate with his contemporaries about how to define the lyric in an Indian language. The range of expressions that native writers have used to describe the nature of the lyric indicates the extent to which they were occupied with this form. In fact, the various native terms for the lyric such as *Sangita Kavya, Atmalakshi Kavya, Swanubhavarasika Kavya, Raagdhwani Kavya, Sangitakalpa Kavya, Urmi Geet, Urmi Kavita* (Divetia 205-6) provide a clue to the range of complex negotiations that took place in the nineteenth century regarding the nature of the lyric form. The process of nativization involved not only the creative adaptation of a Western form but its appropriation in another culture.

Narsinhrao was conscious of the difficulties in adapting an "alien" form for vernacular use: "There are two reasons why it is difficult to find poetry of intense feelings [lyric] in Gujarati literature: One, the context for the poetic evolution of the form was not available on account of the peculiar circumstances of our country and two, forms and metres appropriate for the poetry of intense feeling obtains rarely in our literature, if it exists at all" (66). He argued that the absence of the lyric form in Gujarati poetry made him realize that he had to use the potential of native verse form to suit the poetry of intense feeling, since the Western verse form was not available in his own language (66).

Narsinhrao's engagement with the Romantic tradition and his fashioning of the lyric in Gujarati clearly shows how he tied Romanticism to lyricism and formalism and how this had an enoromous effect on the way romanticism came to be instituted in the native vernacular. He set aside the revolutionary aspect of Romanticism. The romantic ideals of liberty, equality and fraternity never formed a part of the lyric quality that Romantic poetry acquired in the vernacular. It hardly inaugurated a discourse on the common man which it had done in England and elsewhere in Europe. The reason for this could be due to our education under colonialism. It was only with the arrival of Gandhi that the common man came to occupy some space in the literary world of upper caste writers in Gujarat, as elsewhere in India. Leaving aside the problematic nature of Gandhi's intervention, the question which needs to be asked in the context of Narsinhrao's romatic poetry is: Is there something in the nature of colonial rule itself which does not allow the political aspect to emerge at the level of the literary, or is there something in the nature of our caste society in India that it keeps the literary under the grip of a certain formalism and thereby dilutes the question of caste by pushing it out of the domain of literary practice? Edward Said's *Orientalism* (1978) has demonstrated how the west's Romantic preoccupation helped naturalize colonial violence and how it consolidated imperial power. It is, therefore, worth our while to engage with the fact of our Indian/Gujarati Romanticism and the violence it has naturalized in both the colonial and nationalist phase of our history. We might ask, what, for example, was the function and effect of Romanticism in Narsinhrao's poetry and what was the equation it established between the political and the literary?

We might begin by referring to the poem *Rajyarohan* ('Coronation') in which Narsinhrao deals explicitly with a political theme. Written in 1911, it celebrates the coronation of George V as the Emperor of India. Although the poem sets up a tension based on the mutability of dynasties, it remains celebratory in tone and valorizes his kingship:

> Gone are those anxieties, those days of darkness,
> Spreading like peace, the sun has coloured the sky.
> Again, O Delhi! You have donned festive garments,
> And will soon have a new emperor.
>
> In this auspicious hour, pouring happiness,
> Countless drums beat with sweet rhythm, and there
> The suppressed cries of the poor.
> The compassionate king will be able to hear,
>
> In this vast land of Bharat,
> Concealed in the hearts of crores of people,
> The deep feelings of love,
> The loving king will be able to decipher.
>
> Today, the king-emperor,
> Adorns the throne of Bharat.
> But the throne will be still better
> Planted in the hearts of people.
>
> The moment he wears the imperial crown,
> He will forget his kingly comforts.
> He will please the people residing in his heart
> By giving happiness.
>
> By fulfilling the high hopes of people,
> The eager king,
> Will attain to fame eternal
> Cultivating bonds of love.

One can see here the poet's willful, maybe strategic, acceptance of a political order—an acceptance which, at worst, appeals to the goodwill of the colonial masters and, at best, tries to save the soul of poetry from being sullied by the demands of any nationalist politics. In fact, the poet's acceptance of the colonial political order is quite consistent with his universalist poetic ideal. In this respect, he is not much different from Rabindranath

Tagore, who while he professed strong nationalist sympathies, was a votary of the idea of purity in art. In fact, Narsinhrao in his essay "*Kavita ane Rajkiya Sanchalan*" ('Poetry and Political Movements') goes along with Tagore who had said that

> When some storm of a feeling sweeps across the country, art is under a disadvantage. For in such an atmosphere, the boisterous passion breaks through the cordon of harmony and thrusts itself forward as the subject, which with its bulk and pressure, dethrones the unity of a creation (3; original in English).

The "storm of feeling" here clearly refers to the nationalist struggle. Narsinhrao, like Tagore, thinks that the nationalist question is basically a political question, a mere "boisterous passion" which, he thinks, will deprive poetry of "the unity of creation". He argues that "the beauty of poetry is damaged when it is used for political purposes" (3) and that the "treatment of political themes in poetry narrows down our feeling and thinking, whereas poetry which sings of the whole mankind attains universality and width" (5). He further substantiates his argument by drawing from the Sanskrit tradition of Bhavabhuti whose statement "*Amruthaha Atmanaha Kala,*" (the poetry of the soul is eternal) he claims to be the ideal of all poetry. He describes his poetic vocation almost in religio-spiritual terms: "In the face of God's vast creation and the splendour of human existence, the nationalist feelings of a people would certainly look narrow. The poetry which could deal with this theme capably is very rare. The permanence of poetry, therefore, lies in fitting the soul of poetry to the spirit of mankind. Such poetry is only eternal" (6). Again he says, "poetry dwells in the realm of the divine" and has no truck with the "material world" (7). He ends his argument with a rhetorical question: "How can we create poetry consonant with the ideal *Athmanaha Amrutha Kala* in the mean atmosphere of politics, when we know that poetry is divine?" (7).

One could see how Narsinhrao's assessment of poetry in terms of the divine serves two purposes: One, it empties poetry of its historically acquired revolutionary content and pushes it to the domain of the religio-spiritual. Two, it devalues the spirit of nationalism by describing it as a "narrow" and "boisterous passion", capable of damaging the beauty of poetry—beauty consisting in "universality and width", in the singing of "harmony" and "unity". Here, one also sees a careful separation of issues as Narsinhrao constructs the political by setting it up against the literary-aesthetic. He does so by subscribing to a religio-spiritual understanding of poetry where the "eternal" and the "permanent" are held high over the historical here and now. It is, therefore, no surprise that Narsinhrao looks at the political aspect of poetry as a low and narrow aspect of poetic vocation. It is precisely in the context of such an understanding of poetry that the nationalist spirit of his time stands discredited as a form of violence against what he calls the "harmony" and "unity" of creation. The poetic vocation he advocates has very little space for the political and, in fact, it deliberately stays away from the historical here and now.

It is interesting to see how the idea of poetry which Narsinhrao proposes as an antidote to the excesses of nationalism, remains curiously analogous to the nationalist project. Narsinhrao, like many other writers of his generation, tried to bracket the literary-aesthetic away from the political in precisely the way the Congress sought in its early years to bracket the social away from the political. The literary career of Narsinhrao is quite illustrative in the sense that he was one of those poets who lived through two ages of Gujarati poetry. Although he belonged to the *Pandit Yug* (The Age of Scholars), he lived through the *Gandhi Yug* (The Age of Gandhi) in Gujarati literature and was confronted with questions relating to his poetic vocation. It is therefore possible to see in the case of Narsinhrao the ordeal that the poets in Gujarat had to encounter with respect to their vocation with the coming of Gandhian politics and the way they were asked to rearrange their poetic ideal.

In the 1930s, with the advent of Gandhi, a new school of Gujarati writers professing closeness to the people emerged. Coinciding with the emergence of such a school, attacks were launched against Narsinhrao and other writers of his generation on the grounds that they remained alienated from the masses. Narsinhrao defended himself against these charges by arguing that writers like Umashankar Joshi and Kaka Kalelkar, who belonged to the "*Gandhi Yug*" and who were presumably committed to the masses had, in fact, poetic ideals no different from his. He said that Joshi's poetic desire for an expansive, unlimited idea of world peace "is not satisfied with the attainment of a worldly *swaraj*; it is not even content with a world-wide spread of peace; rather it aspires for something still higher, greater" (609). In fact, this aspiration for "something still higher, greater" formed part of a universalist aesthetics, which he thought, was no different from his own. The aesthetics that Gandhi advocated no doubt tried to connect the political with the literary but the literature that was written under his influence was peculiar in its achievements. There is no doubt the poetic vocation and practice in Gujarat had changed immensely with the coming of Gandhi. There was certainly a substantial effort at lodging the political aspect of caste at the centre of literary practice and an attempt at conceptualizing poetry not as "divine" but as a "worldly" practice. But, the writers who followed Gandhi had a religio-spiritual understanding of poetry which formed part of a universalist aesthetics which diluted the aspect of the political and the historical in literature. Such an aesthetics continues to lie at the heart of much of the literary practice in contemporary India, although its hold has weakened considerably on account of challenges coming from dalits, tribal, and women on whose behalf it seeks to speak.

The case of Narsinhrao demonstrates that the literary vernacular, whether fashioned in the colonialist or the nationalist phase, developed an aesthetics which was shaped through a complex engagement with the high tradition of Sanskrit, on the one hand, and the liberal-humanist tradition of the West, on the other. This version of the vernacular still continues to be at the heart of the mainstream educational and literary projects which are supposed to benefit the masses. What I propose in the following section is the staging of a debate around the Sanskritized vernacular in order to show how a vernacular aesthetics based on Sanskrit alienates the very people it tries to espouse and how it marginalizes a whole range of vernacular traditions in the process of its formation.

SECTION IV
THE VERNACULAR AND THE POPULAR: READING TAGORE AFTER ILAIAH

So far in this chapter, I have suggested that the Sanskritizesd vernacular which was brought into being in the nineteenth century was made up of elements drawn from a high tradition of Sanskrit language and literature. I also have suggested that the vernacular aesthetics which was put together at this point of time had caste as one of its major constituents. In fact, we saw how it is the caste component of the vernacular which acts against the democratic urge residing in the vernacular argument. What has rendered the vernacular argument problematic in our time is the inability of the vernacular writer to resolve the question of caste on the one hand and the question of democracy on the other. The reason why the tension between caste and democracy has not erupted as an issue to be debated and discussed in the literary world is perhaps to do with the way the vernacular has so easily constituted itself as the democratic other of the English language. We have become so much used to thinking of the vernacular and the English in oppositional terms that it has become difficult for us to imagine that both these languages have worked as allies in cultivating elitism in India. It was in the nineteenth century that an argument was made in favour of the vernacular and it was pointed out that the educational penetration of the native society could be best achieved through the vernaculars. A systematic effort was made at this time to produce books in the vernacular as it had made a strong claim to the native education programme. The claims of the vernacular, however, were accompanied by a task of producing a suitable language and literature for "modern" education and this could be achieved only through contact with English. Thus, English and the vernacular languages and literatures in India actually worked towards the fulfilment of a similar objective—to consolidate the ideals of universalism and humanism in the native society. The vernacular literatures came to play the role of an ally in disseminating English knowledge among the native population in a way that consolidated the hegemony of the native elite.

The emergence of the vernacular as an ally of the English language and literature needs to be viewed critically. As against the popular perception of the vernacular as an oppositional force, a careful reading of the history of the modern vernaculars in India would reveal that the vernacular, much like English was, another "force" whose potential was exploited for the diffusion of "modern" knowledge in the native society. It would also reveal how both the colonial and the native elite made investments in this "diffusionist" programme of native education. In fact, such an arrangement of education, both in English and in the vernacular, offered the colonial elite the possibility of greater control over the native society. It also helped at the same time the native elite to further their own caste/class interests in the society.

A large body of writing has come out in recent years tracing the various processes through which English language and literature was institutionalized in the native society.[7] But, nothing much has been written about the historical emergence of the vernacular languages and literature, the way they have naturalized themselves in institutions of education. Although it is possible to study the "influence" of English literature on the development of the vernacular languages and literature, it might be more productive to explore the caste/class interests in the native society which brought about an alliance between two seemingly oppositional languages under colonialism. There is no doubt that the interaction between English and the vernaculars were set in terms suitable to both the colonial and native elites but in the process it had put in motion a programme which had enormous consequence for the development of language and literature during the nineteenth century. Scholars have observed how the production of "modern" vernacular literatures marked a "rupture in existing literary practices as well as in the social processes that appear to have been at work transforming the languages and their literatures for centuries." (Tharu 1991 164). The rupture in the literary practices of the vernacular did not simply mean a break with the past; it rather involved a process of "selective marginalization and delegitimization of existing literatures and literary practices, and the constitution of a classical Indian literary tradition" (Tharu 1991 171). It is, therefore, necessary that we examine this history of "marginalized" literatures and literary practices in order to understand the nature and extent of the native elites' investment in the "constitution" of a classical Indian literary tradition. An exercise of this kind, I believe, would dispel our scholarly obsession with a classical past by showing how this obsession has come about on account of colonial and nationlist interventions in the language question. It would also show how what came to be constituted as a a native "tradition" was invented out of a selective appropriation of a classical past and how caste was crucial to the production of vernacular languages and literatures in India.

Writing about the relation between caste and vernacular literatures in India, Sudipta Kaviraj has pointed out that the earlier traditions of vernacular language and literature had "a consciously subaltern relation between themselves and the high classical texts" (1992 34). Citing the example of *bhakti* poetry, he argues that these traditions had worked against "the logic of exclusion of common people from aesthetic and religious seriousness built into the classical Hindu tradition" (1992 34). Traditional Hindu society had a highly literate culture, but that culture thrived on the basis of a "logic of exclusion", thereby limiting the scope of literacy, preventing it from spreading to ordinary unlettered people. The people in the society spoke only vernacular dialects and had no access to a language and a culture which maintained and was maintained by a system of caste prohibitions.

It is through the system of caste that the brahmins had ensured that the skills to master Sanskrit were confined to their own caste. Kaviraj suggests that the caste system came under particular stress on account of the changes brought about by the Muslim rule in India. Although the status of Sanskrit did not diminish under this rule, the entry of both Arabic and Persian languages made a crucial shift in the native perception of language. A mastery of Arabic and Persian was considered essential under the new dispensation. Although the native elite remained tied to Sanskrit on account of the obvious advantages it offered in terms of social authority, they saw in the language of their rulers greater possibilities of control and dominance. Such a change in the native elite's perception of language "continued undisturbed down to the time of Ram Mohan Roy who was proficient in both Sanskrit and Arabic-Persian besides his native Bengali and colonial English" (Kaviraj 1992 32). Despite the intentions of the native elite, Muslim rule created an atmosphere where *bhakti* poetry could flourish and define itself away from the high tradition of Sanskrit. *Bhakti* poetry, which came into prominence in the writings of Nanak, Kabir, Ramanujan and Chaitanya started to undermine the literary and religious hold of Sanskrit. The use of the vernaculars by the *bhakti* poets, Kaviraj shows, marked "an internal conceptual rebellion within classical Brahminical Hinduism": "Bhakti Hinduism, like strands of European Protestantism, sought to destroy the brokerage of the Brahmins between the devotee and his God" (1992 38). This is, of course, not to suggest that the vernacular completely displaced the authority of Sanskrit language and literature. Rather, the historical emergence of the vernacular could be traced to the point when "the vernacular literatures and poetic traditions began an undeclared revolution" (Kaviraj 1992 35) against the supremacy of Sanskrit language and literature.

But such a tradition of the vernacular got increasingly transformed into a "modern" form under British colonialism. Tharu has characterized this "break" as "one in which the principal arenas of literary production shifted from the temple and the court on the one hand and the field or village on the other, to the new port cities: Calcutta, Bombay and Madras" (1991 176). She suggests further that the arrival of the printing press crucially affected the "development" of the vernaculars. Kaviraj has shown that Calcutta, which was an unknown village before the advent of the British, came to acquire a place of eminence and "slowly, the language of the Calcutta *bhadralok* with occasional skillful mixtures from areas which had a reputation for particularly mellifluous accents came to be regarded as the norm language for *bhadralok* Bengalis for all regions of this linguistic area" (1992 44). The making of such a "norm language" was surely related to the emergence of the "written" form of the book.

The use of the vernacular in the book form organized language not only at the material level of letters but elevated the language of the book to an unprecedented supremacy simply by allowing it a greater reach and penetration. Here, I am not suggesting that the "diffusion" of knowledge was made only through the instrument of the book. But what I want to emphasize is that under the circumstances of colonial India a possible diffusion of knowledge among native people was imagined mostly through books. Such a tendency was nowhere as glaringly visible as in the colonial policies on education. For example, every time a case was made for the use of the vernacular in schools and colleges it invariably led to an official stock-taking of books and the case was stalled quite predictably on the ground of the non-availability of books in the vernacular. English decidedly had an advantage over the vernacular in this respect. The arrival of the English book in the native society had created not only hunger for English books but it had also produced among the native community an imperative to produce books in the vernaculars.

The printing press had opened up new opportunities for large-scale production of vernacular books. But uncontrolled proliferation of printed texts posed a problem for the colonial state which had no idea about the kind of effect these books would have in the native mind. It also posed a problem for the native elite whose cultural hegemony had begun to weaken. It is therefore no wonder that the production of books came under surveillance by both the colonial state and the native elite. The colonial rulers could only control the production process by way of censorship, whereas the native elite did it through the criteria of classification. In the context of the publication of Bengali books Tapti Roy has shown how both the colonial state and the native elite had common interests in staking out "criteria of classifying printed literature by *quality* and *taste*" (32; emphasis added).

It is precisely through a careful institution of "quality" and "taste" that the native elite could judge books either as "good" or "bad", "vulgar" or "refined". New rules of taste and respectability were sought not only to define a "high" culture of vernacular literary practice but strict adherence to these rules were also enforced to keep up the moral health of the native population. This clearly was not only a matter of literary taste but was also a matter of politics. The ascertainment of literary taste was one of the tasks which the native elite had to undertake. Almost from the moment this task was formulated there seemed to be two approved sources which the native writers could use for the "improvement" of the vernaculars: One was the "classical" source of Sanskrit language and literature, the other was "modern" English.

The "modernization" of the vernacular was thus envisaged within the limits of Orientalism and Anglicism. Orientalist scholarship which had "retrieved" and put into circulation a large body of classical texts had also created conditions for easy and ready access to knowledge about the Indian past. The Orientalist enterprise which was directed towards the reconstruction of an Indian past was, as Tharu and Lalitha have argued, "a brahminic one in which the Indian society and its history was reduced to what could be found in the ancient sacred texts" (1995 11). Although it is obvious that the methodology which worked only with "the ancient sacred texts" was reductive and partial, the working of such a methodology had produced effects which had become crucial to the making of vernacular literature in the nineteenth century. Tharu and Lalitha argue that "one of the consequences of reaffirming the high brahminical image in the context of a history that was ostensibly in decline was the marginalization of the more recent literatures as well as the literatures that emerged from historically changing, non-brahminical and secular contexts" (1995 11).

Following Tharu and Lalitha it is possible to argue that Orientalism involved processes whereby the Indian past of a perticular order was strategically essentialized as "pure" and "authentic". One can also argue that it was in the nineteenth-century that an essentially brahminized and Sanskritized past was consitituted out of complex history of language and literature in India. Therefore, the claim for an authentic past is as problematic as the claim for its continuity in the present. The advantage of such an argument is that it helps problematize easy associations between "Sanskrit" and "tradition". It brings to the fore the "constructed" character of both these categories. Once Sanskrit is viewed in this manner it no longer remains merely as a "language" or a "literature" but emerges as, to borrow a phrase from Vivek Dhareshwar in the context of the English language, "a juridical/legal apparatus also a political idiom, in short, a semiotic system signifying modernity etc. — to impose its secular categories on the social world" (1993 116). Such a view is defensible once we recognize the extent to which Sanskrit legal texts have been crucial in producing Orientalist knowlege. The Orientalist decision to institute Hindu law on the Sanskrit *shastras* not only led to the enfranchisement of the Hindus as against other communities in India, but it also inscribed brahminical norms into the law-making process. This decision, according to Rosanne Rocher, had "a deep effect on Sanskrit scholarship, in that it led to a renaissance in *dharmasastra* literature" (221). Thus, one can argue that the interest in Sanskrit in the nineteenth century was not merely literary-aesthetic but politico-ideological. Its retrieval as "tradition" was at a moment when a "modern" career was envisaged for Sanskrit. Hastings' decision that "in all suits regarding inheritance, marriage, caste, and other religious usages, or institutions, the laws of the Koran with respect to Mahometans and those of the *Shaster* with respect to Gentoos shall be invariably adhered to" (in Rocher 220) was only the beginning of such career.

One could argue polemically that in the context of nineteeth-century India, Sanskrit as a source language for the improvement of the vernacular was only problematically ancient whereas its functions were modern. What was therefore retrieved as an ancient Indian tradition was an Orientalist construction based on a Sanskritized brahminized and

Hinduized past. Such a tradition was invoked particuarly in the nineteenth century to serve as a model for the betterment of the vernaculars. The other approved model, of course, was English. But as I have suggested in Chapter I, the English model was also of a configuration which had many resemblances to the Sanskrit model. Nevertheless, the status of Sanskrit in relation to English remained ambivalent. On the one hand, Sanskrit-as-tradition was a thing of the past, a reminder to the Hindus of their earlier achievements and subsequent degradation. On the other, Sanskrit-as-modernity had a function similar to English: to improve Hindu society from its present degradation.

It is, however, important to note that the acceptance of this twin Sanskrit-English source for the development of the vernaculars was not total. Although there were efforts at fashioning the vernacular in the image of Sanskrit, such efforts came into conflict with nationalist politics in India and the subsequent need to take the vernacular out of its elite confines and to cast it in the language of the people. During the nationalist phase of its development, the vernacular therefore came to be reconstituted in terms of the "national" and the "popular". In fact, nationalism needed to develop its own critique of the vernacular in order to overcome, on the one hand, the limitations of a foreign language such as English and on the other, the inaccesibility and incomprehensibility of a highly Sanskritized vernacular language and literature. However, as scholars have pointed out, the nationalist projection of the vernacular as popular is to be viewed as part of its politics and not to be treated as "a democratization of the linguistic field" (Kaviraj 1992 45). Since the case for the vernacular was made in the name of the people, it obviously had an democratic agenda but, as Kaviraj has argued, "within its incontestably democratic trends were lodged sharper inequalities of a new kind" (1992 45). Citing the example of Bankim's essay "Bangadeshar Krshak", Kaviraj observes how "the peasantry, the Hashim Sheikhs and Rama Kaivartas of Bankim's famous essay, stood no chance of comprehending the argument in which they figured, and which was made on their behalf—for no other reason but they could hardly understand its Sanskritic grace" (1992 45).

The point is that the popular-vernacular literature of the nationalist variety was part of the burden on nationalist politics to produce a sense of community around language and speech. The construction of a national popular image of the vernacular was, no doubt, crucial from the point of view of the politics which nationalism conducted but it was precisely on account of such a politics that other available critiques of the vernacular were insistently marginalized.[8] In fact, the elite nationalist critiques of the vernacular came both as a response and a counter to the subterranean critiques of elite privilege and monopoly. As a consequence, nationalist invocations of the vernacular were charged and constrained by the necessity to prove that the vernacular was for the people, by the people and of the people.[9]

It is perhaps in this context that it might be useful to examine Rabindranath Tagore's plea for a national education in the vernacular. It is through a reading of some of Tagore's essays on education that I propose to outline the ways in which a link between the vernacular and popular was established and naturalized during the nationalist phase.[10]

In his essay "The Vicissitudes of Education" (1892) Tagore observes that

> "Since our education bears no relation to our life, the books we read paint no vivid pictures of our homes, extol no ideals of our society. The daily pursuits of our lives find no place in those pages, nor do we meet there anybody or anything we happily recognize as our friends and relatives, our sky and earth, our mornings and evenings, or our cornfields and rivers. *Education and life can never become one* in such circumstances, and are bound to remain separated by a barrier" (45, emphasis added).

Tagore's critique of English education derives its force from the separation of "education and life" in the English textbook. There are two reasons, Tagore argues, which make the English book "doubly foreign" to us: "Language is our first difficulty. Because of the many grammatical and syntactical differences between English and our mother-tongue, English is very much a foreign language to us. Then, there is the difficulty connected with the subject matter" (40). Having located the "foreignness" of the English book in terms of language and subject matter he offers the following facts for our consideration:

> Suppose a children's Reader in English contains a story about haymaking and another about a quarrel that Charlie and Katie had when they were snowballing. These stories relate incidents familiar to English children, and are interesting and enjoyable to them; but they rouse no memories in the minds of our children, unfold no pictures before their eyes. Our children simply grope about in the dark when reading these books (41).

Such arguments have become so natural and normal that their continuity in independent India is taken for granted. There is, however, a need to understand how and why such assessments of the English textbook have become powerful.

Tagore recognizes that "the schools in our country, far from being integrated to society, are imposed on it from outside" (68). On the other hand, in Europe, far from being divorced from life, education is "an integral part of it. It grows, develops and circulates in society, and leaves its imprint on what people say, think and do in their everyday life" (68). Such bonding between education in schools and the life outside does not obtain in India where there are "many disagreements, between what [students] learn at school and what their parents and relatives talk about at home" (68). The reason for the failure of the English textbook and the European style of learning, Tagore argues, "need not be sought in any defect in that learning, but in the unfavourable conditions of our life" (46) which precludes the necessary "unity of mind and life and culture" (207). Although it is possible that we might succeed in copying to perfection the externals of the European school "we shall never get the real thing" (58). The "real" thing, according to Tagore, is the harmonization of Indian education with Indian life (69).

How is this unity between education and life to be effected? Certainly not through the imitation of European models. What Tagore proposes is an education based on an understanding of "the ideals by which our country has been attracted and stimulated in the past" (69). He is aware that both European and Oriental learning in their present form are inadequate for the attainment of the "ideals" of the Indian past. Referring to the contemporary system of education, Tagore observes:

> Modern European Culture, whose truth and strength lie in its mobility, comes to us rigidly fixed, almost like our own Shastras, about which our minds have to be passive and uncritical because of their supposed divine origin (208).

Tagore is as critical of modern European knowledge as of the knowledge of the *Shastras*. This is what he says about the culture of the Sanskrit *pathasala*: "it was belauded, as having come straight from Brahma's mouth, or Shiva's matted locks, so that it was unlike anything else in the world, and had to be kept apart and guarded, lest it be contaminated by the touch of the common people" (219). The effect of such an exclusive approach to knowledge, according to Tagore, is that it only allows a foreign language and a foreign culture to have "perfect freedom of movement and growth" (21). The task, therefore, that he recommends to his contemporaries is that of "breaking open the treasure-trove of our ancestors and [of] use [ing] it for our commerce of life" (224). He acknowledges that the present set-up of Hindu society is "letting the Hindu down by smothering his true nature and power" (152).

More than the foreign rule, it is the system of caste, Tagore implies, which is at the root of our educational malady. He maintains that the exclusion of Oriental knowledge from the system of education is one of the reasons why caste has not come under the scrutiny of science. The reason why educated Indians are still under the influence of the pandits and the scriptures, according to Tagore, is that they "study western science at school or college but oriental ones elsewhere in a different milieu" (151), a milieu which forces one into silence by threats of social ostracism when one dares to bring what one learnt at school to bear upon what is outside. The result is the separation between school education and social practice. Although there is a licence to learn Western science, "The strict regulations regarding the licence are calculated to discourage their use" (191). It is therefore necessary to "discard" all customs and prejudices that have kept us "isolated behind artificial barriers" (156). Tagore particularly refers to the manner in which Gokhale's Bill for the introduction of compulsory primary education was received by a section of the educated class in the native society. He locates a self-contradiction among the educated Indians who, while they sent their children to modern schools opposed the extension of the benefits of similar education to the masses. Their opposition, Tagore argues, is not an instance of their "hypocrisy"; "it is simply this: in the soul there has arrived the spring of a new faith, while on the lips the old beliefs still linger" (155). He wants education to spread to the masses but, at the same time, he recognizes the hold social customs and prejudices have on the native mind. The task before us, according to him, is not merely to overcome the language and content of English education but, more important, to overcome the habits of custom and prejudice that prevent education from spreading to the masses.

In Tagore's scheme of education the study of English language and literature is sidelined to "make room for the study of all the languages which carry the living stream of the mind of modern India" (224). To him, through the development of modern Indian languages, knowledge, both Oriental and Occidental, can be made available to a great number of people. He thinks that the issue of the vernacular is closely tied to the issue of mass education. It is the vernacular which can effect the union of education and life, a union which is impossible through an education in English. Tagore argues that " in spite of the great care with which English is learnt in this country, the books that are likely to live a long time are all being written in Bengali" (47). Citing the example of Bankimchandra Chatterji's periodical *Bangadarshan*, he claims that "it was the instrument with which a great genius broke down the barrier between our education and our life and effected the joyous union of our head and heart" (46). The reason for *Bangadarshan*'s mass appeal, Tagore argues, was not because it produced truth earlier unknown, but it "made us see ourselves in a new, revealing light. In the figures of Suryamukhi and Kamalamani, it showed our women as they are; in the characters of Chandrasekhar and Pratap, it raised the ideal of Bengali manhood; and it cast a ray of glory on the petty affairs of our day-to day life" (47). What characterized *Bangadarshan* was its "universality" which was consistent with "the world literary trends". (134).

In Tagore's scheme of things the vernacular was poised between English and Sanskrit: like English it could carry the Western knowledge of the world and unlike Sanskrit it could carry the living stream of folk tradition back home, admitting no barrier between caste and caste, the learned and the unlearned. Therefore, it was found to be the fit vehicle for bridging the gap between "education and life". Post-Independence conceptualizations of mass education continue to invoke such a function for the vernacular. To cite one example, Moturi Satyanarayana a post-Independence educationist, in his essay "Common Language as a Functional Vehicle and Its Place in Education" refers to Tagore's notion of the vernacular while taking stock of the linguistic policies adopted in independent India:

> The language of the region today is the sole educational medium throughout India upto high-school standard with a few exceptions here and there...the country's decision in this respect has not only been firm but irreversible. With the formation of linguistic state [sic] the implementation of this decision has been accelerated. Rabindra Nath Tagore once said: "in no country in the world except India is to be seen this divorce between the language of education from the language of people" (54-55).

Kancha Ilaiah in his *Why I Am Not a Hindu* (1996) invokes precisely this disjunciton between education and life. More than a hundred years after Tagore's "The Vicissitudes of Education", Ilaiah describes education in independent India in terms astonishingly similar to Tagore's. However, his account of this disjunction is made in the context of a vernacular education offered by the Indian state as a part of its commitment to democratize education. The question to be asked then is: How is it that a vernacular education which Tagore so strongly advocated and which the Indian state so promptly implemented as a means to bridge the gap between education and life could produce a similar gap?

Ilaiah raises the issue of vernacular education in a powerful way in his book *Why I Am Not a Hindu*. Here, he suggests that there is a need to rethink the vernacular question. According to him, language like other civil-social institutions, is a significant arena where caste confi cts are staged. Giving the example of school textbooks, he says:

> As we were growing up, stepping into higher classes, the textbooks taught us stories which we had never heard in our families. The stories of Rama and Krishna, poems from the Puranas, the names of the two epics, *Ramayana* and *Mahabharata* occurred repeatedly. Right from early schools upto college, our Telugu textbooks were packed with these Hindu stories. For Brahmin–Baniya students these were their childhood stories very familiar not only in the story form but in the form of the Gods they worshipped.... I distinctly remember how alien all these names appeared to me. Many of the names were not known in my village. The name of Kalidas was as alien to us as the name of Shakespeare. The only difference was that one appeared in Telugu textbooks, while the other appeared in English textbooks (13).

Ilaiah shows through a systematic analysis how the "production-based communicative language" (13) of the Dalitbahujan is written out of school textbooks. The standardized, Sanskritized Telugu of the school textbook is not, he argues, "merely a difference of dialect; there is difference in the very language itself" (13), indeed they represent two cultures. Showing how Dalitbahujan "homes have one culture and the schools have another culture" where "the textbook language was against [the Dalitbahujan]," Ilaiah further argues:

> What difference did it make to us whether we had an English textbook that talked about Milton's *Paradise Lost* or *Paradise Regained*, or Shakespeare's *Othello* or *Macbeth* or Wordsworth's poetry about nature in England, or a Telugu textbook which talked about Kalidasa's *Meghasandesham*, Bommera Potanna's *Bhagavatam* or Nannaya's and Tikkana's *Mahabharatam* except the fact that one textbook is written with twenty six letters and the other in fifty

> six letters? We do not share the contents of either; we do not find our lives reflected in their narratives. We cannot locate our family settings in them. In none of these books do we find words that are familiar to us without the help of a dictionary. Neither makes any sense to us. How does it make any difference to us whether it is Greek or Latin that are written in Roman letters or Sanskrit that is written in Telugu (15).

The above passage contests the idea of a standardized and Sanskritized form of the vernacular which in post-Independence India has come to be accepted as "popular". In fact, Ilaiah's description of the alienation felt by the Dalitbahujan in the context of vernacular textbooks resonates with the alienation that Tagore locates in the predicament of the Bhadralok Bengali boy's relation with the English textbook. It also renders problematic Tagore's easy conflation of the vernacular with the "national" and the "popular". A caste reading of the vernacular such as Ilaiah's questions the nature of the vernacular which is institutionalized in independent India, a vernacular which alienates the very "masses" it aims to integrate.

Tagore is clearly aware of the link between caste and education. He characterizes caste as an evil to be overcome in order for the Hindu to "secure a special kind of fulfillment for humanity, a level of perfection that must be a gain for all" (131). His essentially humanitarian project, therefore, visualizes a generous sharing of "*Our* religious and social customs", "*Our* places of worship", "*Our* ancient lore" (132, emphasis added). He could therefore construct a tolerant Hinduism which could make space for Islam and Christianity (131). He could also powerfuly argue against the caste system: "If we stand aloof in our 'purity', passing on this pride of isolation to succeeding generations, if we make our religion and social customs exclusively our own, our places of worship forbidden to outsiders and our ancient lore kept under lock and key, then we shall simply proclaim to the world that we have been condemned to death in the court of humanity" (132). This expansive humanism which engenders a throwing open of ancient lore, hitherto forbidden, to the "masses" is definitely at the heart of Tagore's vernacular project. But, the vernacular born out of such an impulse to democratize does nothing but consolidate what Ilaiah calls brahminical knowledge informed as it is by Sanskritic traditions that are central to caste privileges. Ilaiah contends that vernacular education in independent India continues to be an area where caste privileges are reinforced and modernized in the name of democracy.

NOTES

1. Sister Nivedita, the American disciple of Swami Vivekananda, was closely associated with the Ramakrishna Mission. Influential in her time and after, she was described by Rabindranath Tagore as having "uttered the vital truths about Indian life" in his introduction to her book *The Web Of Indian Life* (1917). In the subsequent section, I have focussed on a compilation of her writings on education: *Hints on National Education in India* (Calcutta: Udbodhan Press, 1967).
2. All quotations except wherever specified are translations from the original Gujarati. Translations mine.
3. For example, see his "*Kavita Ane Sangit*," *Kavithavichar* (Bombay: R.R. Sheth, 1969) 8-75.
4. For a statement about his poetic vocation see *Kavithavichar*, 211-2.
5. Critics such as Umakant Joshi and Balwant Rai have also made similar comments. See Joshi et al., *Gujarati Sahityano Ithihas*, Vol. 3 (Ahmedabad: Gujarati Sahitya Parishad, 1978) 363.
6. See, for example, "*Kavitha Ane Sangit*" and "*Gujarati Sahityama Sangit Kavya*," *Kavithavichar*, 8–75 and 166–204 respectively.
7. See, for example, Svati Joshi, ed., *Rethinking English: Essays in Literature, Language, History*, (New Delhi: Trianka, 1991); Rajeswari Sunder Rajan, ed., *The Lie of the Land: English Literary Studies in India*, (New Delhi: Oxford UP, 1993); Susie Tharu, ed., *Subject to Change: Teaching Literature in the Nineties*, (New Delhi: Orient Longman, 1998).
8. See, for example, V. Geeta's reading of the works of Ayothidas Panditar, and E.V. Ramaswamy Periyar in "Re-writing History in the Brahmin's Shadow: Caste and the Modern Historical Imagination," *Journal of Arts and Ideas* 25-26 (1993): 127–137.
9. See, for example, Partha Chatterjee's reading of Bankimchandra in *Nationalist Thought and the Colonial World: A Derivative Discourse*? (New Delhi: Oxford UP, 1986) 78.
10. All references to Rabindranath Tagore's essays are from his collection *Towards Universal Man* (Bombay: Asia, 1961).

Four

English in a Democratic Nation

SECTION I
ENGLISH AND THE DEMOCRATIZATION OF EDUCATION

In the previous chapter I have shown how the vernacular came to be constituted in the image of English and how in the nationalist phase the English language came to be characterized as alien and elitist against the native vernacular. I have also demonstrated how the mainstream focus on the English-vernacular debate over medium of instruction successfully deflected attention from caste critiques and their focus on access to education. These subaltern caste critiques, I argue, kept their focus on the monopoly exercised by specific castes over education. They raised questions about any easy conflation of education with merit. Using caste as an entry point into the constitution of an English-led vernacular, I showed how the claim of the vernacular to have fused education with life was problematic and how caste remained and even now remains as a powerful constituent of vernacular language and literature in India.

Several complex transformations occured in English education as a result of its changing relationship with the vernacular in the nationalist phase. The diffusionist role envisaged for the vernacular in colonial education policy was refigured in the nationalist phase in a manner which allowed a modernized and popularized version of the vernacular to emerge as a challenge to English education. Education in the vernacular came to be pitted increasingly against education in English because the latter had a greater appeal in the context of a national education policy commited to the ideals of democracy. As against colonial arguments which had envisaged a wholesale importation of European knowledge to the colony, the nationalist characterizations of English education involved a more pragmatic and instrumental borrowing. It is at this juncture, I argue, that the teaching of English in India was split into a debate over language and literature.

The language issue in postcolonial India took shape in the context of a fierce debate over what should constitute the national language.[1] The nationalist desire for the democratization of education through the vernacular was written into the constitution. It was envisaged that English would be dropped in education and other spheres after 15 years of independence. However, the intense language debates of the 1960s led inexorably to the consolidation of English as the language of higher education. Broadly, it was agreed that the mother tongue was to be the language of school education on account of its proximity to life and that English was to be the language of college education by virtue of its role as the bearer of modernity. Such a conceptualization of education had two effects. One, it characterized the vernacular as the wellspring of democracy as well as the repository of tradition, a tradition which English would harness and modernize for national progress. Two, the separately imagined domains of English and the vernacular set up a field where democracy and modernity were marked off from each other.

However, the focus on the debates over the medium of instruction in the first two decades after Independence obscured the fact that the structure of education remained largely intact. The procedure which conferred merit and certified efficiency continued to rest in a system of education organized laterally in terms of a prescribed series of courses and graded hierarchically into school and college education. In the second chapter we saw how the notion of merit came to be premised on a liberal-humanist idea of the autonomous individual and how it served to erase a history of privileged access to education enjoyed by dominant castes. One consequence of the retention of such structures in independent India has been that education, whether vernacular or English, continues to be the site where merit is manufactured. By extension, higher education is cast as the realm of higher merit. Since the realm of higher education is equally the realm of English, English came to be the mark not only of modernity but of merit.

The nationalist commitment to the democratization of education, no doubt, extended the sphere of education and educational opportunity. But, it also subtly instituted an unequal relation between education in the vernacular and education in English. The inequality in their relationship consisted in the fact that a vernacular education was considered incomplete without an education in English. Although English seemed to have lost its struggle against the vernacular as a medium of instruction in Independent India, it continued to feature prominently as a major course component in a system of education which worked through the vernaculars. It was not only taught as "literature" but an entire new career for English was envisaged through a systematic "language" learning programme to enable the vernacular medium student access to higher education in English.

It was in this context that a policy decision was made soon after Independence to introduce a new type of English course which subsequently was naturalized as "Compulsory English".[2] For example, the study group appointed by the Ministry of Education, Government of India reiterated in 1967 that "Compulsory English should be taught, not merely in the first and second year of the three year degree course, but for all the three years" (in Loomba 28). The reason which was given for its consolidation was that "this makes for better comprehension of written materials in English—a skill which is essential as ever at the post-graduate stage" (in Loomba 28). The implication of this injunction was that whatever be the medium of instruction at the school level, Compulsory English had to be studied for all the three years at the udergraduate level. The idea of a Compulsory English course was tied to the idea of the question of equipping the undergraduate students with language skills necessary to access higher education. The underlying assumption was that access to advanced levels of learning is possible through English alone. Although the vernacular medium was thought adequate for laying the foundational principles of various disciplines it does not fulfill adequately the requirements of higher levels. It was argued that students needed to equip themselves with enough competence in English to acquire advanced knowledge. It is perhaps for this reason that Compulsory English has become the most widely taught undergraduate course in India. Indeed, it is almost impossible to acquire a graduate degree without passing a Compulsory English course in contemporary India.

It is, therefore, important to note that a "compulsory" course in English carries a national mandate in the sense that it is one of the "choices" exercised by the Indian nation-state as part of its effort to commit English, however lowly, to the greatest number of Indian people. Viewed in this manner, this course seems to be one of the forms which English has taken in order to accomodate the democratic urges of the Indian state. In fact, it is a course which carries the burdens of both the processes of democratization and modernization—a complex process which neither an education in the vernacular nor in English can alone hope to accomplish. The questions then are: Does the Compulsory English course actually offer students the competence and skill that it is supposed to? Does it fulfill its promise of democratizing higher education? Does it really offer the vernacular medium student access to the world of English? The urgency of these questions can be made out from the way the vernacular medium student feels let down by his/her Compulsory English course which hardly delivers the linguistic competence it promises.

However, my concern here is not to emphasize the failure of the course, rather it is to ask what exactly does a course in Compulsory English accomplish, what does it consolidate and what "function" does it serve in our education system. It is clear that the terms in which this course was put together had to do, on the one hand, with a nationalist desire to utilize the vernacular as a popular medium of education and on the other, with an intenton to make English available to the greatest number of people so that it becomes free from its configuration as an elitist language. The putting together of a Compulsory English course involved a difficult process. In their effort to fashion such a course its proponents were mostly driven by the nationalist critiques of English language and literature. It is in this context that a reading of a few Compulsory English textbooks produced in independent India could be useful. Concentrating largely on their "Editorials", "Prefaces" and "Introductions", the most neglected parts of the language text books, I hope to show how anthology-making is not a simple and an innocent act of putting together a few lessons but involves an activity which is not merely literary-aesthetic but politico-ideological.

SECTION II
RETHINKING COMPULSORY ENGLISH

The three-year Compulsory course at the undergraduate level has always an "anthology" at the first year level. The course which usually starts with an anthology of short stories and essays invariably culminates in the teaching of a literary text, either a novel or a play. For example, during 1998-99 the undergraduate Compulsory English course for Commerce students of Gujarat University, Ahmedabad has an anthology *Jubilee English Reader* for the first year; Ruskin Bond's novel *The Room on the Roof* for the second year and Henrik Ibsen's play *The Pillars of Society* for the third year of study. It is in the context of such a course that the teaching of English as a language remains inseparable from its teaching as literature. The role of literature in a predominatly language oriented course such as "Compulsory English" however remains fraught with tension. Nationalist critiques of English language and literature inevitably worked to devalue the place which English literature used to enjoy in the colonial system of education. But these nationalist critiques, as I pointed out earlier in the book, were framed within a logic which upheld the signifcance of literature as a bearer of universal humanist values. Such a logic in post-

Independence India was harnessed to expand the boundaries of literature to include in English language anthologies, not only English authors but Indian writers in English as well. It is however noteworthy that Indian writers had already become part of the anthologies produced for Indian students in pre-Independence India. For example, one could take the anthology entitled *Ten Tales: For Indian Students* published in 1931. The popularity of this text could be gauged from the fact that it went through seven reprints, sometimes twice in a year, in a span of thirteen years. Out of the ten short stories included in this anthology four are by Indians: "The Babus of Nayanjore" and "The Castaway" by Rabindranath Tagore; "The Letter" by Gaurishanker Joshi and "The Muscular Son-in-law" by Prabhat Kumar Mukhopadhyay. The inclusion of these Indian writers seems natural and normal in the context of the Arnoldian conceptualization of literature as an expansive space without national boundaries, a space where a Tagore can jostle unproblematically alongside Frederick Marryat, Anatole France and Leo Tolstoy. The logic which underwrites this collection of short stories and bestows unity on writers of diverse national origins and of divergent themes and styles can be gleaned through the way the book is introduced to its readers:

> The characters and incidents of the story may be drawn from any grade of society, from the upper classes, from the middle classes, or from the lower classes, for the essentials of human life and character are the same in every class.
>
> The incidents or even the characters may take a special colour from the age in which they are supposed to be placed or the country or even the particular community to which they are supposed to belong. Such special colour adds a special interest to the story. But here again the essential human elements are the same and that is why we find real interest in these stories. (*Ten Tales* iv)

It is evident that such a logic based on the "essentials of human life and character" works inevitably towards the production of a universalist notion of literature. The operational logic of such an anthology is that "age", "country" and "community" are no bar in the reading and appreciation of literature and that the proper provenance of literature is not any specific society or class but the essentials of human life which is assumed to be the same everywhere. Such a notion of literature remains the basis for many of the selections of material for anthologies. For example, the editor of *Selected Prose Models* (1985) declares in the "Preface" that

> These models of well-written prose represent a cross-section of the best that has been thought and said in English in our century. The writers chosen for this anthology are master spirits who have freely drawn upon the genius of the English language, or to whom the theme matters as much as the idiom, or whose thoughts have an enduring appeal. (Augustine n.p.)

Another editor, D.P. Patnaik, while introducing the anthology *Sense and Sensibility* (1964) announces that the selection is designed to

> give a bird's eye view of the development of English prose from the eighteenth century to the twentieth, with an emphasis upon the prose of today. They are also taken from the writings of different lands to bring home to the young students the richness and cosmopolitan character of English prose. The book offers not only a variety of styles, but aslo a diversity of interests and subject matter—embracing almost the entire gamut of human experience (iii).

That the production of an anthology is not an isolated activity and that it is crucially related to the institutional structures can be observed from the way Patnaik envisages a career for his anthology:

> The purpose of education is to produce a total man—one who is aware of and sensitive to the varied aspects of life. It is hoped that this anthology will help in that process by opening before its readers new vistas of beauty and wonder (iv).

The function which Patnaik assigns to the anthology is clear: to produce "a total man". Further, he believes that such a function could be accomplished by acquainting the readers with the writings of different lands and ages. He also believes that the cosmopolitan character of English prose would not only give its reader access to the entire gamut of human experience but would also make him sensitive to the varied aspects of life.

The editors of *Popular Short Stories* (1988) accept the cosmopolitan character of English language but differ in their selection of material. The explanation which they provide for their selection procedure is as follows:

> This collection of short stories mainly focuses on characters and situations familiar in modern life. Many readers cannot appreciate stories that gave delight to an older generation. The types of schools and law courts that Dickens, for instance, describes in his novels are relics of the past; his Victorian characters are difficult to recognize in a modern situation. Young people today therefore find that those novels do not communicate with them personally. We hope that this selection of narratives of situations and description of persons from modern society will appeal and relate to young readers (*Popular Short Stories n.p.*).

This collection, in accordance with the declared intentions of its editors, includes stories only by twentieth-century authors. The underlying assumption is that stories by modern authors would strike a personal chord in the heart of its readers as they would instantly recognize the characters and situations as their own. The editors do recognize a split between modern education and modern life, but they believe that this split could be overcome through a reading based on modern authors, and not from reading the writers of the past.

The need to unite education and life is also a major preoccupation in these anthologies, *Links: Indian Prose in English* (1989), the editor, G.S. Balarama Gupta makes a selection from Indian non-fictional prose writings in English spanning nearly two centuries. He argues that Indian prose writings in English antedate those in verse and are numerous enough to constitute a significant body of Indian literature in English. It is through a collection of such writings that Gupta wants to present "a complex of values––educational, ethical, spiritual and cultural—which Indian historical experience and heritage uphold" (v). He further declares that

> Our purpose in publishing an anthology comprising Indian non-fictional prose writing in English is to offer such specimens of English prose as would help Indian readers to respond to them more inclusively than they would to those of Western writings having cultural overtones alien to their experience or sensibility (ix).

One could see that the various attempts to use "literature" as part of a Compulsory English course reveal an area of contest where the "alienness" of English literature is stressed and a certain authenticity is claimed for Indian writing in English. Although the values of English literature are challenged on the ground of lack of authenticity, the universalist and humanist descriptions of literature are retained. Indian writers and their works are claimed to be representative of a way of life that can be easily recognized as "Indian". These literature-oriented textbooks seem to be constantly defining Indian material as more authentic and therefore more suitable for the education of Indian students. Apart from this authenticity argument which seems to put Indian writing in English in opposition to English literature, what is most striking about these textbooks is their wholesale recognition that a "literary" education is the best possible education, the difference between the value of an education based on Indian literary material and the one based on "alien" and "foreign" material being only a difference in degree. The claim is that the Indian material would serve the purpose of bridging the gap between education and life "more" efffectively than the material based on "western writings having cultural overtones alien to [Indian] experience or sensibility". But, as I have argued in the context of the relationship between caste and vernacular literature, writing based on Indian experience and Indian languages could be as alienating as Western writings. By extending this argument one could claim that a literary text, whether Indian or Western, vernacular or English, can be alienating to a person coming from a dalit background.

The development of a caste perspective on literature, I believe, would help us to grasp some of the unquestioned assumptions that have gone into the making of many literature-oriented textbooks. But since these textbooks are part of a course oriented mainly towards teaching English as a language, the literature aspect of the course is taught in the most unproblematic manner. Despite the apparent variety of these textbooks they are structured by an almost uniformly designed set of exercises which are usually appended to the "lessons".

The status of literature in a language-oriented Compulsory English course, however, is very tenuous. It has always been countered by a certain aggressive "functionalism" which is reflected in many textbooks. *The Romance of Living*, a textbook published in 1962, puts this conflict into perspective in its "Preface":

> On the one hand, there are the new, and perhaps legitimate, demands for functional prose as reading material; on the other, there is the equally valid belief that the reading material can be used for training, enlarging and disciplining the consciousness of the young reader. It is difficult to reconcile these opposing attitudes, and the preparation of an anthology, therefore, involves a lot of self-examination (Singh n.p.).

Such a posing of the problem in terms of an opposition between language and literature, between functional prose and literary prose, only prefigures a theme which has since then become a major point of discussion in the official policy on English education. A committee appointed in 1967 to report on the study of English in India held that a demarcation of language and literature teaching would serve the nation best. It also predicted that

> More and more students are sure to opt for language study, for that is the need of the hour. We expect that within the next twenty years or so, most of the departments of English in the Universities will have changed over mainly to a language oriented post-graduate course in English (in Loomba 28).

While it is possible to argue that the prediction has not come true and that the Departments of English have not changed over to language-oriented post-graduate courses, it is certainly important to emphasize that a decision in favour of "functionalism" is definitely not unrelated to a certain decline of interest in English literature courses in postcolonial India.

In fact, the stress on the utilitarian aspect of English education is quite consistent with the developmental logic of the nation-state. It is also clear that more and more students are in fact opting for language study. The popularity of private English language tuition classes and courses also bear testimony to a clear preference for the teaching of English as a language.[3]

Within the academy, the expression of this utilitarian attitude to English can be located in the production of language-oriented textbooks and their popularity in independent India. For example, the editors of *Twentieth Century English Prose* (1986), while taking stock of the textbooks produced in the past, state the following in their "Preface":

> For some time past, there has been a shift of emphasis from the study of literature to the acquisition of communication skills in English at the undergraduate level. In consequence, language oriented prose texts have come out in plenty (Department of English, Kashmir University iii).

The argument that English is a skill to be acquired is certainly a part of the managerial and bureaucratic approach to national growth. Such an approach is crucially linked to the Nehruvian model of development which relies on science and technology for the transformation of India from a backward, underdeveloped nation into a developed one. In a scheme which marks a shift from the cultural to the economic, from the Humanities to I.T., English comes to be refigured in terms of its contemporary utility value. This is of course not to suggest that English education was ever free from a certain utilitarianism. Rather it is to reiterate that in the context of a national commitment to science and technology, the need to develop innovative courses in English literature have become a challenge. Many contestants have emerged in independent India to take its place, Indian writing in English is one, apart from Commonwealth and American literature, which have effectively occupied the pride of place earlier accorded to English literature. English has no longer remained English. In fact, as I have argued elsewhere in the book, it never was. But, in our time, the claim of English over literature has been considerably reduced. It is quite obvious from the changing configuration of the English literature syllabus in the last fifty years. The English literature course in post-Independence India has become more diverse. However the expansion of the syllabus through inclusion of other national literatures and literature from marginalized groups should not be seen as a democratization of the literary field. Rather it should be seen as symptomatic of a crisis in literary studies signifying a crisis in civil society. Further, in this phase, as Sunder Rajan has argued, English as a language has "developed into an international commodity with a privileged connection with the English nation" (14).

The function of Compulsory English was clearly to transform a vernacular education at school to an English-oriented education at college in the interest of a nation committed to science and technology. In this respect, Compulsory English was a product of a nationalist offer to democratize the leadership and management of the state. Equally, it was the product of a logic that worked with the assumption that English alone held the key to the cutting edge of research in science and technology. Since competence in English language was seen to be crucial to the highest levels of research and therefore, by extension, to the nation-building project, the splintering of English into language and literature courses profoundly refigured the Compulsory English course. Charged with the task of producing "competence" in the English language, the Compulsory English anthology struggled with a variety of conceptualizations designed to offer an instrumental grasp of the language to those who did not have it.[4] To raise the question of competence is, however, to raise the question of standards. Therefore, even as the Compulsory English course is constructed in terms of a democratic offer, it is simultaneously considered as a guardian of standards, a gateway to the higher reaches of education and to elite spaces within the nation-building process.

The dual function of Compulsory English appears to open out two related sets of questions. On one hand, questions could be asked about the efficacy of the course—whether it genuinely offers a competence in English, or fulfills its democratic obligation to allow a vernacular medium student access to college education. On the other hand, another set of questions could be asked about its evaluative function which polices access to higher education, constructs new forms of merit, certifies new types of efficiency.

These new forms of merit, complicit with a competence in English, are powerfully linked to the nation-building process.

As I have argued in the second chapter, the notion of merit was a contentious one, employed by the nationalist elite to counter the "Depressed Class" demands for proportional representation in government services. The equation of competence in English with merit is therefore also linked to the question of caste. Compulsory English, which institutes a rigorous uniformity in its pedgogical practices, operates on the assumption that students everywhere are alike. This notion of homogenization of the student body erases all differences of class, caste, community and gender. The pedagogical practices premised upon uniform standards of courses are loaded in favour of the elite groups, disempowering precisely those students to whom a democratic offer is made. Therefore, it is possible to argue that the effects of the movement from English literature teaching in the colonial phase to English language teaching in the postcolonial phase did not in any considerable way dismantle the construction of education as a site for the production of an elite class of Indians. In fact, one can argue that the function of a scientific English language education, like that of a humanist literary education, is to fashion and consolidate the elite. Although literary studies and language studies have been imagined as significantly distinct, the fact that the Compulsory English anthology often sets up an easy conflation of the two suggests that their function and effects are not dissimilar: to consolidate elitism in India. The Compulsory English course, which on the face of it seems to resist the configuration of English as an elite language, in fact undermines its own offer by being caught in an education system committed to the establishment of a relationship of equality between an English and vernacular education.

Viewed in this manner, the introduction of a Compulsory English course in Independent India seems to be the logical outcome of a role that was envisaged for English in a predominantly vernacular-driven education system. The need to reorganize English at the undergraduate level on a "compulsory" basis reflects, on one hand, the burden of English for a vernacular system of education and on the other, a reassertion of the value of English. Thus, the Compulsory English course is the one which not only shows the limits of a vernacular system of education but it is also the one through which a vernacular-led education tries to overcome its limits. For example, the editors of *An English Anthology for College Classes* (1968) write in their "Foreword" about how they "became aware of the enormous gap between how much English a student who sought admission to a college really knew and how much he ought to have known". On the basis of such a realization they argued that "It would not help matters if we merely sat back and blamed the secondary schools. We, therefore, decided to do whatever we could to improve the conditions of English teaching at this level" (*An English Anthology* iii).

From the above analysis it is clear that language teaching in the shape of Compulsory English course is structured more in relation to the politico-ideological than the literary-aesthetic. Nevertheless, there has been very little recognition of the politics of a Compulsory English. Somehow there is an assumption that it is possible to continue with the business of English without getting into the politics of language and literature. But such assumptions are actually enmeshed in the politics of our time. For example, one argument made frequently in the context of a structural adjustment programme and the economics of liberalization and globalization is about the potential value of English in a market-driven global economy. As C.K. Seshadri has argued, "India has signed the WTO ageement and has become a part of the global knowledge based economy. Most of this knowledge is available in English. It is time our professors came out of their ivory towers of theory and literary criticism, and tackled the real problems of teaching English, unless they want to be swept off their feet by swift winds of change" (209). Such a market-oriented approach to English, which seems to be consistent with our time, carries echoes of the predictions made in 1967 in the report submitted by the study group appointed by the Ministry of Education, Government of India. In fact, Seshadri's argument is in line with the suggestion made in the report regarding the desirability of introducing language-oriented post-graduate courses in Indian universities. Seshadri, for example, argues that "if there can be departments of French, German or Russian which teach these "languages" at the university level, one fails to understand why the English language cannot be taught" (206). A language-oriented course at the university level, it is believed, would solve the problem of teaching at the school and college level. Such a belief issues out of his realization that "most teachers of English in schools are products of our university system. Obviously, our departments of English do not equip them with the kind of skills needed to teach English!" (Seshadri 206). At least one funciton of such a skill-based argument in favour of English is to requisition existing infrastructure to the services of the market. Although the needs of the market are not necessarily consistent with those of the nation-state, this argument successfully uses English to unproblematically conflate one need with the other. Moreover, such arguments work with the assumption that good teachers with improved skills and innovative ideas could ensure effective teaching of English. This argument reiterates the logic of language studies which figures efficiency in terms of better teachers, better textbooks, better syllabus and better courses.

The question one would like to ask here is: why does the ground reality in the classroom as well as in the surrounding educational environment remain the same, despite strenuous efforts at the level of policy formulation, curriculum design, syllabus making, textbook production and a variety of other inputs? No doubt, there is a sense of satisfaction at the expert specialist level of the profession. But, nagging evidences keep surfacing. Having taught for several years in rural Gujarat and having worked with batch after batch of students who pass their Compulsory English course without acquiring the competence that it is meant to offer, I am convinced that the severe mismatch between what is intended and what is found at the end of a course cannot be reduced to the inadequacy of the textbook, teacher or methodology. Yet, language teaching in India continues to be structured around a confidence that efficiency in teacher training, production of textbooks and methodologies could successfully produce competence in English. The basic premise of this reformist logic seems to be that intentions based on sound pedagogic principles can match the reality on the ground. The Acharya Rammurthy Commission Report of 1990 observes that eleven English language institutes exist but standards vary and the overall standards of English are going down. However, it seeks to address this problem by recommeding the use of technology for language development (in Chatterji 306).

Such procedures, rcommendations, and suggested improvements serve to homogenize the student body and to erase differences of caste, community and gender. By calling for a pedagogical emphasis on the ideal of the national progress, these recommendations elide the notion of education as a terrain of struggle, a field which fosters critical consciousness. Disregarding the relationship of knowledge and power, refusing to acknowledge the political aspect of education, they assume that the teaching of English is an innocent activity concerned with the imparting of reading, writing and communicative skills. Such a market-oriented pedagogical thrust, as I have shown through my reading of the anthology editorials, is itself undewritten by an ideology which consolidates the space of the elite by arbitrating standards of competence in English, no matter whether it is taught as a language or a literature or as both.

In present-day India, it appears that interventions which bring questions of class, caste, community and gender back into the classroom might enhance teaching practices. Besides, the recognition that notions of skill and standard are ideological could open out alternative ways of conceptualizing education, be it in English or in the vernacular.

NOTES

1. See G. Sundara Reddi, ed., *The Language Problem in India,* (New Delhi: National, 1973) and S.N. Mazumdar, *Marxism and the Language Problem in India,* (New Delhi: People's Publishing House, 1970) for a comprehensive account of divergent views on the issue of national language during the first two decades after Independence.
2. The course "Compulsory English" is also called "General

English" in some Indian Universities.

3. As an index of popular demand for such private courses, refer to the bilingual *Rapidex English Speaking Course*, (New Delhi: Pustak Mahal, 1998) 16th edition. This course is available in twelve Indian languages and claims to have five crore readers.
4. For example, there are efforts at designing separate courses for students of Commerce and Science with the assumption that the interests of commercial and scientific topics would stimulate the language learning process. G.C. Thornley, the editor of *Easier Scienticfic English Practice* (New Delhi: Longmans, 1964) writers that the book is "a first collection of writing of scientific interest" which would "provide those who are interested in Science with material for fairly easy practice in English language" (vii). Similarly, R.K. Khanna et al. in their anthology *English for Students of Commerce* (New Delhi: Oxford UP, 1991) state that "most of the essays are on topics of interest to students of Commerce" in order to "meet their [language] needs" (n.p.).

Conclusion

There is no doubt that the question of language and education remains entangled in contemporary India. The nationalist resolution of the language question in favour of the vernacular has become fragile and seems to have lost its utility. A binary logic which works only to demonize English and which valorizes the vernacular within a comfortable structure of "alien" and "native" seems no longer sustainable. There seems to be an urgent need to reimagine the modern vernacular which we have shaped so caringly in our immediate nationalist past. The task seems to be enormous given the emotional investment that has gone into the making of the vernacular languages and literatures in India. However, there is no doubt that the modern and liberal values that the nationalist elite has cultivated so carefully in the vernacular literatures in India have become controversial at this point of time, particularly in the face of the challenge that Dalit thought, for example, has posed to the vernacular in India.

My contention is that the questioning of modern and liberal values would demand nothing less than the questioning of the elite self, the way it has organized itself since the time of nationalism, particularly in relation to caste but equally in relation to questions of gender and community. This book, therefore, has made a conscious endeavour to work outside the English–vernacular divide in order to examine how vernacular education in India, much like education in English, has become a major site of power and privilege. One of the real effects of pitting the vernaculars against English in India has been that it has kept the domain of education from being perceived as the preserve of a caste, class or community. Working across the binary of the English and the vernacular would enable us to develop frames through which we might be able to enquire into the historical processes that have shaped the national/regional forms of the vernacular. Such an enquiry would also help dismantle a powerful nationalist discourse that has constructed the idea of "the mother tongue" in a way that refutes any interrogation of the vernacular. The discourse around "the mother tongue" has created such an aura around the language question that we continue to cast the modern, regional vernacular as a "popular" form of language even while we know that it continues to constitute itself solidly along caste and class lines.

A historically grounded understanding of the vernacular demands that we look at the emergence of our languages and literatures more critically without giving in too easily to the trappings of a universalist aesthetics which works with the idea of the "universal" and the "human". We need to understand that such a form of aesthetics has evolved historically in the conditions of nineteenth-century colonial India and that the upper caste elite which remained at the vanguard espoused this particular form of aesthetics which banished questions of caste and class from the world of literature. It is in the context of a threat to their own caste and class privileges that the native elites forged an aesthetics out of the universalist and humanist elements of a classical, brahminical past, much in the manner in which the colonial elite constructed an aesthetics of "high seriousness" out of the elements of an enlightened European past when confronted with the working class literature in England. Vernacular studies in India, therefore, must recognize that such an aesthetics based on essential humanism is born out of a historical reluctance on the part of the elite to accommodate "caste" and "class" as categories of valid aesthetic engagement. In fact, our vernacular humanism is only as large and as liberal as our caste system.

National education in India has been significantly underwritten by a liberal-humanist ideology. Caste and class interests have found a quiet shelter here. The national elite, educated in such a system of education, has grown to believe that questions of caste and class are only distractions on our way to become human. The challenge before us is to bring the questions of caste and class back into our national consciousness and not allow them to rot in our unconscious, thinking that our modernity and our nationalism have somehow resolved these questions and that they are redundant in contemporary India. We need to develop a pedagogy that allows critical consciousness to emerge out of an engagement with questions of caste and class.

The nationalist resolution of the language question in favour of the vernacular during our anti-colonial struggle has consecrated it to such an extent that its meaning and value has become a matter of faith, something as if beyond doubt. We have not only imbibed this nationalist burden but we have also turned this defence of the vernacular into a nationalist task, even when we know that the vernaculars are aligned against the forces of democracy in India. Since Indian nationalism has configured the vernacular as "democratic" and as "popular" by projecting it against the alien character of English, we have somehow come to believe that a questioning of the vernacular would be against the interest of the nation. However, a time has come when we need to rethink the nationalist vernacular imagination which is being increasingly challenged by the forces of democracy in India. Now, it seems as if the questions of caste and class, which we thought we had somehow managed to resolve in our nationalist past, have come back to haunt us as the unresolved elements of our imagination.

The vernaculars in India must reconsider their role in the education system. What has become clear in the last fifty years of education in India is that the use of the vernacular has not ensured the democratization of education; it has only perpetuated the caste/class domination of the elite through a selective use and deployment of the vernacular resources of the country. One could perhaps cite the arrival of the greatest number of people at the site of education as a sign of the democratization of the educational field but it turns out to be only the empty signifier of a process, particularly in the face of the continuing elite dominance in the field of education. The national elite remains singularly unmindful to the benefits that have accrued to it on account of its continuing access to education. There seems to be a complete lack of critical consciousness on the part of the elite to engage with its own privileges in society.

An absence of self-reflexivity on the part of the elite has led time and again to grave civil-social crisis in India. The anti-Mandal agitation is only one glaring example where one came to see how the caste and class elite in India came together to produce a self-assured discourse on "salvaging the nation" and defended the idea of "merit", "competence" and "standard" in education, pushing questions of caste privilege and continuing access to education out of the field of their conceptual engagement. In this, both the English and the vernacular elite spoke the same language and were no different on their position on the issue of caste-based-reservation in education. Therefore, the argument that the English-educated elite has somehow triumphed over the limitations of caste and that the vernacular elite continues to be under its spell is not historically defensible. In fact, the actions of the caste and class elite in India continues to be more collaborative than oppositional even though this elite is visibly divided along the binaries of the English and the vernacular, the modern and the traditional. Our modernity, much like our traditionalism is constituted powerfully by our caste interests and there is no doubt that the language question in India is ultimately about caste.

Bibliography

Acharya, Poromesh. "Bengali 'Bhadralok' and Educational Development in 19th Century Bengal." *Economic and Political Weekly* 30.13 (1995): 670-3.

Advani, Shalini. "Educating the National Imagination." *Economic and Political Weekly* 31.31 (1996): 2077-82.

Agnihotri R.K and A.L. Khanna. *Problematizing English in India.* New Delhi: Sage, 1997.

Ahmad, Aijaz. *In Theory: Classes, Nations, Literatures.* New Delhi: Oxford UP, 1992.

________. *Lineages of the Present: Political Essays.* New Delhi: Tulika, 1996.

________. "The Politics of Literary Postcoloniality." *Contemporary Postcolonial Theory.* Ed. Padmini Mongia. New Delhi: Oxford UP, 1997.

Aloysius, G. *Nationalism without a Nation in India.* New Delhi: Oxford UP, 1998.

Ambedkar, B.R. "Statement Concerning the State of Education of the Depressed Classes in the Bombay Presidency." 1928. *Writings and Speeches.* Vol. 2. Comp. and ed. Vasant Moon. Bombay: Education Department, Government of Maharashtra, 1982. 405–428.

________. "A Report on the Constitution of the Government of Bombay Presidency." 1929. *Writings and Speeches.* Vol. 2. Comp. and ed. Vasant Moon. Bombay: Education Department, Government of Maharashtra, 1982. 315–401.

________. "Speech at the Plenary Session of the Third Round Table Conference." 1930. *Writings and Speeches.* Vol. 2. Comp. and ed. Vasant Moon. Bombay: Education Department, Government of Maharashtra, 1982. 503–509.

________. "Proceedings of the Sub-Committee No. VI (Franchise), Second Sitting." 1930a. *Writings and Speeches,* Vol. 2. Comp. and ed.

Vasant Moon. Bombay: Education Department, Government of Maharashtra, 1982. 557–578.

———. "Note to the Indian Franchisee Committee." 1932. *Writings and Speeches.* Vol. 2. Comp. and ed. Vasant Moon. Bombay: Education Department, Government of Maharashtra, 1982. 491–500.

———. *What Congress and Gandhi Have Done to the Untouchables.* 1945. *Writings and Speeches.* Vol. 9. Comp. and ed. Vasant Moon. Bombay: Education Department, Government of Maharashtra, 1991.

———. *Dr. Babasaheb Ambedkar: Writings and Speeches.* Vols. 1–14. Comp. and ed. Vasant Moon. Bombay: Education Department Government of Maharashtra, 1979-1995.

———. *Annhilation of Caste.* 1936. New Delhi: Arnold, 1990.

———. *Emancipation of the Untouchables.* 1943. Bombay: Thacker, 1972.

Amin, Shahid. *Event, Metaphor, Memory: Chauri Chaura, 1922-1992.* New Delhi: Oxford UP, 1995.

Anderson, Benedict. *Imagined Communities.* London: Verso, 1996.

An English Anthology for College Classes. Bombay: Macmillan, 1968.

Anyon, Jean. "The Retreat of Marxism and Socialist Feminism: Postmodern and Poststructuralist Theories in Education." *Curriculum Inquiry* 24.2 (1994): 115–133.

Arnold, Matthew. "The Study of Poetry." 1853. *The English Critical Tradition.* Vol.2. Eds. S. Ramaswami and V.S. Sethuraman. Madras: Macmillan, 1978. 63–89.

———. "The Choice of Subjects in Poetry." 1864. *The English Critical Tradition.* Vol.2. Eds. S. Ramaswami and V.S. Sethuraman. Madras: Macmillan, 1978. 1–16.

———. "The Function of Criticism in the Present Time." 1880. *The English Critical Tradition.* Vol. 2. Eds. S. Ramaswami and V.S. Sethuraman. Madras: Macmillan, 1978. 17–43.

Auckland, Lord. "Minute." 1836. *Selections from Educational Records 1781-1839.* Comp. and ed. H. Sharp. 1920. New Delhi: National Archives of India, 1965. 147.

———. "Minute." 1839. *Selections from Educational Records 1781-1839.* Comp. and ed. H. Sharp. 1920. New Delhi: National Archives of India, 1965. 147–170.

Augustine, A.E., ed. *Selected Prose Models.* Madras: Macmillan, 1985.

Bagchi, Jasodhara. *Gem-like Flame: Walter Pater and the Nineteenth Century Paradigm of Modernity.* Calcutta: Papyrus, 1997.

Baldick, Chris. *The Social Mission of English Criticism.* Oxford: Clarendon, 1983.

Bapuji, B.R. *Society, State and Education: Essays in the Political Sociology of Language Education.* Madras: T.R. Publications, 1993.

Basu, Aparna. *The Growth of Education and Political Development in India, 1898-1920.* New Delhi: Oxford UP, 1974.

Batsleer, Janet et al., eds. *Rewriting English: Cultural Politics of Gender and Class.* London: Methuen, 1985.

Bauman, Emily. "Re-dressing Colonial Discourse: Postcolonial Theory and the Humanist Project." *Critical Quarterly* 40.3 (1998): 79–89.

Bayley E.C. "Letter to the Secretary of the Government of Punjab." 1868. *Selections from Educational Records of the Government of India: The Development of University Education 1860-87.* Ed. J.P. Naik. New Delhi: National Archives of India, 1963. 39–44.

_______. "Letter to the Secretary of the Government of Punjab." 1869. *Selections from Educational Records of the Government of India: The Development of University Education 1860-87.* Ed. J.P. Naik. New Delhi: National Archives of India, 1963. 55–58.

_______. "Minute on the Proposed Modifications in the Calcutta University System." 1870. *Selections from Educational Records of the Government of India: The Development of University Education 1860-87.* Ed. J.P. Naik. New Delhi: National Archives of India, 1963. 96–106.

_______. "Minute of Dissent on the Proposal for Raising the Punjab University College to the Status of University." 1877. *Selections from Educational Records of the Government of India: The Development of University Education 1860-87.* Ed. J.P. Naik. New Delhi: National Archives of India, 1963. 219–224.

Bayly, C.A. *The New Cambridge History of India: Indian Society and the Making of the British Empire.* Cambridge: Cambridge UP, 1988.

Belsey, Catherine. "Literature, History, Politics." *Modern Criticism and Theory.* Ed. David Lodge. London: Longman, 1988.

Bergonzi, Bernard. *Exploding English: Criticism, Theory, Culture.* Oxford: Clarendon, 1990.

Bethune, J.E.D. "Letter to Dalhousie" 1850. *Selections from Educational Records 1840-1850.* Comp. and ed. J.A. Richey. 1922. New Delhi: National Archives of India, 1965. 52–56.

Bhabha, Homi. *The Location of Culture.* London: Routledge, 1994.

_______. ed. *Nation and Narration.* London: Routledge, 1995.

Bhattacharya, Sabyasachi, ed. *The Contested Terrain: Perspectives on Education in India.* New Delhi: Orient Longman, 1998.

Bloom, Harold. *The Western Canon: The Books and Schools of the Ages.* London: Papermac, 1995.

Boman–Behram, B.K. *Educational Controversies in India.* Bombay: Taraporevala, 1946.

Bose, A.M. "Memorial Opposing the Proposed University for the Punjab." 1881. *Selections from Educational Records of the Government of India: The Development of University Education 1860-87.* Ed. J.P. Naik. New Delhi: National Archives of India, 1963. 309–11.

Bourdieu, Pierre. *Outline of a Theory of Practice.* Cambridge: Cambridge UP, 1982.

Boutros, F. "Extract from 'An Enquiry into the System of Education most likely to be generally Popular in Behar and the Upper Provinces.'" 1842. *Selections from Educational Records 1840-1859.* Comp. and ed. J.A. Richey. 1922. New Delhi: National Archives of India, 1965. 5–11.

Breckenridge Carol A. and Peter Van Der Veer, eds. *Orientalism and the Postcolonial Predicament.* New Delhi: Oxford UP, 1994.

Chadha, Tara et al., eds. *A Foundation English Course for Undergraduates: Reader I.* New Delhi: Oxford UP, 1985.

Chakrabarty, Dipesh. "An Invitation to a Dialogue." *Subaltern Study IV.* ed. Ranajit Guha. New Delhi: Oxford UP, 1985.

———. "Modernity and Ethnicity in India: A History for the Present." *Economic and Political Weekly* 30.52 (1995): 3365–72.

Chander, Jagdish, ed. *Creative English.* Madras: Oxford UP, 1976.

Chandra, Sudhir. *The Oppressive Present: Literature and Social Consciousness in Colonial India.* New Delhi: Oxford UP, 1992.

Chatterjee, Kalyan K. *English Education in India: Issues and Opinions.* New Delhi: Macmillan, 1976.

Chatterjee, Partha. *Nationalist Thought and the Colonial World: A Derivative Discourse?* New Delhi: Oxford UP, 1986.

———. *The Nation and Its Fragments.* New Delhi: Oxford UP, 1994.

———. "The Disciplines in Colonial Bengal." *Texts of Power: Emerging Disciplines in Colonial Bengal.* Ed. Partha Chatterjee. Calcutta: Samya, 1996. 1–29.

———. ed. *Texts of Power: Emerging Disciplines in Colonial Bengal.* Calcutta: Samya, 1996.

———. *A Possible India: Essays in Political Criticism.* New Delhi: Oxford UP, 1998a.

———. *The Present History of West Bengal: Essays in Political Criticism.* New Delhi: Oxford UP, 1998.

———. "Community in the East." *Economic and Political Weekly* 33.6 (1998): 227–82.

——— and Gyanendra Pandey, eds. *Subaltern Studies VII.* New Delhi: Oxford UP, 1992.

Chatterji, Lola. "Landmarks in Official Educational Policy: Some Facts and Figures." *The Lie of the Land.* Ed. Rajeswari Sunder Rajan. New Delhi: Oxford UP, 1993.

Cohn, Bernard. *An Anthropologist among the Historians and Other Essays.* New Delhi: Oxford UP, 1990.

Coomaraswamy, Ananda K. *Essays in National Idealism.* New Delhi: Munshilal Manoharlal, 1981.

Corefield, Penelope. J., ed. *Language, History and Class.* Oxford: Basil Blackwell, 1991.

Crittenden, Brian. "Conflicting Traditions and Education in a Democracy: Can Liberalism Provide Defensible Common Values?" *Curriculum Inquiry* 24.3 (1994): 293–326.

Crowley, Tony. *Proper English?: Readings in Language, History and Cultural Identity.* London: Routledge, 1991.

Dalhousie, Lord. "Letter." 1850. *Selections from Educational Records 1840-1859.* Comp. and ed. J.A. Richey. 1922. New Delhi: National Archives of India, 1965. 62.

Department of English, The University of Kashmir, eds. *Twentieth Century English Prose.* New Delhi: Oxford UP, 1986.

Devy, G.N. *After Amnesia: Tradition and Change in Indian Literary Criticism.* Bombay: Orient Longman, 1992.

_______. *In Another Tongue: Essays on Indian Literature in English.* Madras: Macmillan, 1995.

Dhareshwar, Vivek. "Caste and the Secular Self." *Journal of Arts and Ideas.* Special Number on Careers of Modernity. 25-26 (1993): 115–126.

_______. " 'Our Time': History, Sovereignty and Politics." *Economic and Political Weekly* 30.6 (1995): 317–24.

_______. "Postcolonial in the Postmodern: Or, the Political after Modernity." *Economic and Political Weekly* 30.30 (1995): 104–12.

Dighe, Anita. "Deconstructing Literacy Primers." *Economic and Political Weekly* 30.26 (1995): 1559–61.

Divetia, Narsinhrao B. *Kavitavichar.* Ed. Bhriguraj Anjaria. Bombay: R.R. Sheth, 1969.

D'Souza, Austin A. *Anglo-Indian Education: A Study of Its Origins and Growth in Bengal upto 1960.* New Delhi: Oxford UP, 1976.

Eagleton, Terry. *Criticism and Ideology.* London: Verso, 1978.

Economic and Political Weekly. Special Number on Secularism, Modernity and the State. 29.28 (1994).

Ellenborough, Lord. "Letter to the Court of Directors." 1858. *Selections from Educational Records 1840-1859.* Comp. and ed. J.A. Richey. 1922. New Delhi: National Archives of India, 1965. 131–134.

Elliott, C.A. "Letter to the Registrar of the Calcutta University." 1870. *Selections from Educational Records of the Government of India: The Development of University Education 1860-87.* Ed. J.P. Naik. New Delhi: National Archives of India, 1963. 115–120.

Elphinstone, W.F. et al. "Letter from the Court of Directors to the Governor-General in Council of Bengal." 1814. *Selections from*

Eductional Records 1781-1839. Comp. and ed. H. Sharp. 1920. New Delhi: National Archives of India, 1065. 22–24.

"Extract from the Despatch from the Court of Directors, East India Company to Government of India." 1854. *Selection from Educational Records 1840-1859.* Comp. and ed. J.A. Richey. 1922. New Delhi: National Archives of India, 1965. 127–130.

Foucault, Michel. *The Archaeology of Knowledge.* London: Tavistock, 1977.

———. *Discipline and Punish: The Birth of the Prison.* New York: Vintage, 1979.

———. "What is Enlightenment?" *A Foucault Reader.* Ed. Paul Rabinow. Harmondsworth: Penguin, 1984.

Freire, Paulo. *Pedagogy of the Oppressed.* New York: Seabury, 1970.

———. *Education for Critical Consciousness.* New York: Continuum, 1989.

Giroux, Henry A. *Schooling for Democracy: Critical Pedagogy in the Modern Age.* London: Routledge, 1989.

Gokak, V.K. "Speech at the Plenary Session." *The Teaching of English Literature Overseas.* Ed. John Press. London: Methuen, 1963. 27–34.

Goodman, Sharon and David Graddok, eds. *Redesigning English: New Texts, New Identities.* London: Routledge, 1996.

Gordon, David. "Education as Text: The Varieties of Educational Hiddenness." *Curriculum Inquiry* 18.4 (1988): 449–467.

Gramsci, Antonio. *Selections From Prison Notebooks.* Ed. and trans. Quentin Hoare and Geoffrey Nowell Smith. Hyderabad: Orient Longman, 1996.

Grant, Charles. Extract from "Observations on the State of Society among the Asiatic Subjects of Great Britain, particularly with Respect to Morals; and on the Means of Improving it." 1797. *Selections from Educational Records 1781-1839.* Comp. and ed. H. Sharp. 1920. New Delhi: National Archives of India, 1965. 81-86.

Guha, Ranajit. "On Some Aspects of the Historiography of Colonial India." *Subaltern Studies I.* Ed. Ranajit Guha. New Delhi: Oxford UP, 1982. 1–7.

———. "Dominance Without Hegemony and its Historiography" *Subaltern Studies VI.* Ed. Ranajit Guha. New Delhi: Oxford UP, 1989. 210–309.

———. ed. *A Subaltern Studies Reader 1986-1995.* New Delhi: Oxford UP, 1998.

Guidelines to the Universities for Preparation of Development Proposals for the Seventh Plan. New Delhi: University Grants Commission, 1986.

Gupta, G.S. Balrama, ed. *Links: Indian Prose in English.* Madras: Macmillan, 1989.

Gupta R.S. and Kapil Kapoor, eds. *English in India*. New Delhi: Academic, 1991.

Habib, Irfan. *Interpreting Indian History*. Shillong: North-Eastern Hill UP, 1985.

________. *Essays in Indian History: Towards a Marxist Perception*. New Delhi: Tulika, 1995.

Halliday, F.J. "Letter to the Government of Bengal." 1850. *Selections from Educational Records 1840-1859*. Comp. and ed. J.A. Richey. 1922. New Delhi: National Archives of India, 1965. 58–60.

Halsey, A.H. et al, eds. *Education: Culture, Economy and Society*. Oxford: Oxford UP, 1997.

Hardiman, David. *Peasant Nationalists of Gujarat; Kheda District, 1917-1934* New Delhi: Oxford UP, 1981.

Harrington J.H. et al. "Letter from the General Committee of Public Instruction to the Governor-General, Fort William." 1824. *Selections from Educational Records 1781-1839*. Comp. and ed. H. Sharp. 1920. New Delhi: National Archives of India, 1965. 93–98.

Harris, Kevin. *Education and Knowledge*. London: Routledge and Kegan Paul, 1979.

Hashmi, Syed Mashroor Ali Akhtar. *Muslim Response to Western Education: A Study of Four Pioneer Institutions*. New Delhi: Commonwealth, 1989.

Haynes, Douglas E. *Rhetoric and Ritual in Colonial India: The Shaping of a Public Culture in Surat City, 1852-1928*. Berkeley: U of California P, 1991.

Howell, A.P. "Education in British India, 1870-71." 1872. *Selections from Educational Records of the Government of India 1859-1871*. Vol: I. Ed. A.M. Monteath and A.P. Howell. New Delhi: National Archives of India, 1960.

Howell, M.S. "Note on the Media of Instructions in Schools." 1868. *Selections from Educational Records of the Government of India: The Development of University Education 1860-87*. Ed. J.P. Naik. New Delhi: National Archives of India, 1963. 67–74.

Hutchinson, John and Anthony D. Sith, eds. *Nationalism*. Oxford: Oxford UP, 1994.

Ilaiah, Kancha. *Why I Am Not a Hindu*. Calcutta: Samya, 1996.

Illich, Ivan. *Celebration of Awareness: A Call for Institutional Revolution*. Harmondsworth: Penguin, 1972.

________. *Deschooling Society*. Harmondsworth: Penguin, 1973.

Inglis, Fred. *The Management of Ignorance: A Political Theory of Curriculum*. Oxford: Basil Blackwell, 1985.

Jain, Manju and Frances B. Singh, eds. *Today: Modern Prose for College Students*. New Delhi: Macmillan, 1981.

Jervis, Colonel. "Minute." 1847. *Selections from Educational Records 1840-1859*. Comp. and ed. J.A. Richey. 1922. New Delhi: National Archives of India, 1965. 11–14.

John. V.V. *The Great Classroom Hoax and Other Reflections on India's Education*. New Delhi: Vikas, 1978.

Joshi Svati, ed. *Rethinking English: Essays in Literature, Language, History* New Delhi: Trianka, 1991.

Joshi, Umashankar, A. Raval and Yashwant Shukla, Eds. *Gujarati Sahityano Itihas*. Vol. 3. Ahmedabad: Gujarati Sahitya Parishad, 1978.

Journal of Arts and Ideas. Special Number on Representations in History. 17-18 (1989).

Journal of Arts and Ideas. Special Number on Careers of Modernity. 25–26 (1993).

Journal of English and Foreign Languages. Special Number on Teaching Literature. Ed. Susie Tharu. 7–8 (1991).

Jussawalla, Adil and Eunice De Souza, eds. *Statements: An Anthology of Indian Prose in English*. Bombay: Orient Longman, 1976.

Kapferer, Judith. "Structured Social Inequalities." *Curriculum Inquiry* 16.1 (1986): 1–31.

Kaul, Suvir. "The Indian Academic and the Resistance to Theory". *The Lie of The Land: English Literary Studies in India*. Ed. Rajeshwari Sunder Rajan. New Delhi: Oxford UP, 1993.

Kaur, Kuldip. *Education in India (1781-1985): Policies, Planning and Implementation*. Chandigarh: CRRID, 1985.

Kaviraj, Sudipta. "Writing, Speaking, Being: Language and the Historical Formation of Identities in India." Unpublished manuscript. 1992.

———. *The Unhappy Consciousness: Bankimchandra Chattopadhyaya and the Formation of Nationalist Discourse in India*. New Delhi: Oxford UP, 1998.

Kejariwal, O.P. *The Asiatic Society of Bengal and the Discovery of India's Past, 1784-1838*. New Delhi: Oxford UP, 1988.

Kempson, M. "Letter to the Secretary to the Government of the North-Western Provinces." 1869. *Selections from Educational Records of the Government of India: The Development of University Education 1860-87*. Ed. J.P. Naik. New Delhi: National Archives of India, 1963. 81–85.

Khanna, R.K. et al., eds. *English For Students of Commerce*. New Delhi: Oxford UP, 1991.

King, Robert D. *Nehru and the Language Politics of India*. New Delhi: Oxford UP, 1997.

Kopf, David. *British Orientalism and the Bengal Renaissance: The Dynamics of Indian Modernisation 1773-1835.* Berkeley: U of California P, 1969.

Krishnasamy, N. and T. Sriraman, eds. *Current English for Colleges* Madras: Macmillan, 1995.

Kumar, Krishna. *The Social Character of Learning.* New Delhi: Sage, 1989.

_______. *The Political Agenda of Education.* New Delhi: Sage, 1991.

Kurup, P.N. Keshava and B. Ardhanareeswaran, eds. *New Patterns of Contemporary Prose.* Madras: Macmillan, 1978.

Liston, Daniel, P. *Capitalist Schools: Explanation and Ethics in Radical Studies of Schooling.* New York: Routledge, 1988.

Littler, J.H. "Minute." 1850. *Selections from Educational Records 1840-1859.* Comp. and ed. J.A. Richey. 1922. New Delhi: National Archives of India, 1965. 57.

Lohia, Rammanohar. *Language.* 1956. Hyderabad: Rammanohar Lohia Samata Vidyalaya Nyas, 1986.

Loomba, Ania, "Criticism and Pedagogy in the Indian Classroom." *The Lie of the Land: English Literary Studies in India.* Ed. Rajeswari Sunder Rajan. New Delhi: Oxford UP, 1993.

Macaulay, T.B. "Minute." 1835. *Selections From Educational Records 1781-1839.* Comp and ed. H. Sharp. 1920. New Delhi: National Archives of India, 1965. 107–117.

Macleod, D. "Minute on the Proposal for the Establishment of a University at Lahore." 1869. *Selections from Educational Records of the Government of India: The Development of University Education 1860-87.* Ed. J.P. Naik. New Delhi: National Archives of India, 1963. 51–55.

Mahmood, Syed. *A History of English Education in India, 1781-1893.* 1895. New Delhi: Idarah-i Adabiyat-i Delli, 1981.

Mani, Lata. "The Production of an Official Discourse on Sati." *Europe and Its Others.* Vol. 1. Ed. Francis Barker et al. Colchester: U of Essex P, 1985.

Marathe, Sudhakar, et al., eds. *Provocations: The Teaching of English Literature in India.* Hyderabad: Orient Longman, 1993.

Marshall, G.T. "Report on the Sanskrit College, Benares." 1841. *Selections From Educational Records 1840-1859.* Comp. and ed. J.A. Richey. 1922. New Delhi: National Archive of India, 1965. 254–256.

Marshall, P.J. *The New Cambridge History of India: Bengal, The British Bridge Head, Eastern India 1740-1828.* Cambridge: Cambridge UP, 1987.

Mazumdar, Satyendra Narayan. *Marxism and the Language Problem in India.* New Delhi: People's Publishing, 1970.

Mazumdar, Vina. *Education and Social Change.* Shimla: Indian Institute of Advanced Study, 1972.

McGuire, John. *The Making of a Colonial Mind: A Quantitative Study of the*

Bhadhralok *in Calcutta, 1857-1885.* Canberra: Australian National UP, 1983.

McCully, Bruce. *English Education and the Origins of Indian Nationalism.* New York: Columbia UP, 1942.

McMurty, J. *English Language and English Literature.* London: Mansell, 1985.

Mehd, Susmita. *Narsinhraono Kavya Kusum.* Bombay: Macmillan, 1960.

Menon, Dilip M. "Caste and Colonial Modernity: Reading *Saraswativijayam.*" *Studies in History* 13.2 (1997): 291–312.

Mishra, D.S. and R.S. Jadeja, eds. *Stories for India.* Madras: Macmillan, n.d.

Moira, Lord. "Minute on the Judicial Administration of the Presidency of Fort William." 1815. *Selections from Educational Records 1781-1839.* Comp. and ed. H. Sharp. 1920. New Delhi: National Archives of India, 1965. 24–29.

Monteath, A.M. "Note on the State of Education in India." 1862. *Selections from Educational Records of the Government of India 1859-71.* Vol. I. Eds. A.M. Monteath and A.P. Howell. New Delhi: National Archives of India, 1960.

———. "Note on the State of Education in India, 1865-66." 1867. *Selections from Educational Records of the Government of India 1859-71.* Vol. I. Eds. A.M. Monteath and A.P. Howell. New Delhi: National Archives of India, 1960.

Mookerjee, I.C. et al. "Petition of the British Indian Association, North-Western Provinces." 1867. *Selections from Educational Records of the Government of India: The Development of University Education 1860-87.* Ed. J.P. Naik. New Delhi: National Archives of India, 1963. 25–28.

Mukherjee, L. *Problems of Administration of Education in India.* Allahabad: Kitab Mahal, 1960.

Mukherjee, Meenakshi. *Realism and Reality: The Novel and Society in India.* New Delhi: Oxford UP, 1980.

Nair, V. Gopalan and S. Velayudhan, eds. *Contemporary Prose for Degree Classes.* Madras: Oxford UP, 1980.

Naik, J.P. ed. *Selection from Educational Records of the Government of India: The Development of University Education 1860-87.* New Delhi: National Archives of India, 1963.

Nambissan, Geetha B. "Language and Schooling of Tribal Children: Issues Related to Medium of Instruction." *Economic and Political Weekly* 29.42 (1994): 2747–54.

Nandy, Ashis. *The Illegitimacy of Nationalism: Rabindranath Tagore and the Politics of the Self.* New Delhi: Oxford UP, 1994.

Narsimhamurthy, M.G., Ed. *Stories British and American.* Hyderabad: Orient Longman, 1976.

Nayar, M.G., ed. *Highlights of Modern English Prose.* Madras: Macmillan, 1992.

Niranjana, Tejaswini. *Siting Translation: History, Post-structuralism and the Colonial Context.* Hyderabad: Orient Longman, 1995.

______. "Questions for Cultural Politics." *Subject to Change: Teaching Literature in the Nineties.* Ed. Susie Tharu. New Delhi: Orient Longman, 1998.

Nivedita, Sister. *Hints on National Education in India.* Calcutta: Udbodhan, 1967.

Oliphant, J. et al. "Educational Despatch No. 49." [Wood's Despatch] 1854. *Selections from Educational Records 1840-1859.* Comp. and ed. J.A. Richey. 1922. New Delhi: National Archives of India, 1965. 364–393.

Omvedt, Gail. *Dalits and the Democratic Revolution: Dr. Ambedkar and the Dalit Movement in Colonial India.* New Delhi: Sage, 1994.

Orsini, Francesca. "What Did They mean by 'Public'?: Language, Literature and the Politics of Nationalism." *Economic and Political Weekly* 34.7 (1999): 409–416.

Palshikar, Suhas. "Gandhi-Ambedkar Interface: ...When Shall the Twain Meet?" *Economic and Political Weekly* 31.31 (1996): 2070–5.

Panikkar, K.N. *Culture, Ideology, Hegemony: Intellectuals and Social Consciousness in Colonial India.* New Delhi: Tulika, 1995.

Paranjape, Makarand, ed. *Nativism: Essays in Criticism.* New Delhi: Sahitya Akademi, 1995.

Patnaik, D.P., ed. *Sense and Sensibility: A Prose Anthology for University Students.* Bombay: Orient Longman, 1964.

Pennycook, Alastair. *The Cultural Politics of English as an International Language.* London: Longman, 1994.

Perry, E. "Minute." 1847. *Selections from Educational Records, 1840-1859.* Comp. and ed. J.A. Richey, 1922. New Delhi: National Archives of India, 1965. 14–16.

"Petition of the Students of the Government Sanskrit College of Calcutta." 1836. *Selections from Educational Records, 1781-1839.* Comp. and ed. H. Sharp. 1920. New Delhi: National Archives of India, 1965.

Poddar, Arabinda. *Renaissance in Bengal: Quests and Confrontations, 1800-1860.* Shimla: Indian Institute of Advanced Studies, 1970.

Popular Short Stories. New Delhi: Oxford UP, 1988.

Prabhakar, T., ed. *Frontiers of Prose.* Madras: Macmillan, 1986.

Radice, William, ed. *Swami Vivekananda and the Modernization of Hinduism.* New Delhi: Oxford UP, 1998.

Rai, Lajpat. *The Problem of National Education in India*. 1920. New Delhi: Ministry of Information and Broadcasting, Government of India, 1967.

Ramakrishnan, E.V. *Making it New: Modernism in Malayalam, Marathi and Hindi Poetry*. Shimla: Indian Institute of Advanced Study, 1995.

Ramaswami, S. and V.S. Sethuraman, eds. *The English Critical Tradition*. Madras: Macmillan, 1978. 2 vols.

Rao, H.G. Suryanarayana, ed. *Prose for Pleasure and Comprehension*. Madras: Oxford UP, 1981.

Rapidex English Speaking Course–Gujarati. Trans. Sashikala Trivedi. New Delhi, Pustak Mahal, 1998. 16th Edn.

Ratcliff, A.J.J., ed. *Stories and Essays: A Selection from Nineteenth and Twentieth Century English Prose*. London: Oxford UP, 1954.

Reddi, G. Sundara, ed. *The Language Problem in India*. New Delhi: National, 1973.

Rees, R.J., *English Literature: An Introduction for Foreign Readers*. Madras: Macmillan, 1973.

Reid, H.S., "Note on the Necessity of Establishment of a University for North India." 1868. *Selections from Educational Records of the Government of India: The Development of University Education 1860-87*. Ed. J.P. Naik, New Delhi: National Archives of India, 1963. 74-80.

"Report on Public Instruction in Bengal 1849-50." 1850. *Selections from Educational Records 1840-1859*. Comp. and ed. J.A. Richey. 1922. New Delhi: National Archives of India, 1965. 60-61.

Richey, J.A., comp. and ed. *Selections from Educational Records 1840-1859*. 1922. New Delhi: National Archives of India, 1965.

Rocher, Rosane. "British Orientalism in the Eighteenth Century: The Dialectics of Knowledge and Government." *Orientalism and the Postcolonial Predicament*. Eds. Carol A Breckenridge and Peter Van Der Veer. New Delhi: Oxford UP, 1994.

Roy, Rammohan. "Letter to the Governor General in Council." *Selections from Educational Records 1781-1839*. Comp. and ed. H. Sharp. 1920. New Delhi: National Archives of India, 1965. 99–101.

Roy, Tapti. "Disciplining the Printed Text: Colonial and Nationalist Surveillance of Bengali Literature." *Texts of Power*. Ed. Partha Chatterjee. Calcutta: Samya, 1996. 30–62.

Rudolph, Susan H. and Lloyd Rudolph, eds. *Education and Politics in India*. New Delhi: Oxford UP, 1972.

Said, Edward. *Orientalism*. New York: Vintage, 1979.

Sarkar, Sumit. *A Critique of Colonial India*. Calcutta: Papyrus, 1985.

_______. *Writing Social History*. New Delhi: Oxford UP, 1997.

Satyanarayana, Moturi. "Common Language as a Functional Vehicle and Its Place in Education." *The Language Problem in India*. Ed. G. Sundara Reddi. New Delhi: National, 1973. 52–62.

Seal, Anil. *The Emergence of Indian Nationalism: Competition and Collaboration in the Later Nineteenth Century India*. Cambridge: Cambridge UP, 1971.

Sebastian, D.K., ed. *Prose for the Young Reader*. Madras: Macmillan, 1985.

Seshadri, C.K., "English Studies in India." *Critical Theory: Western and Indian*. Ed. P.C. Kar. New Delhi: Pencraft, 1997.

Sharp. H., comp. and ed. *Selections from Educational Records. Vol. I. 1781-1839*. 1920. New Delhi: National Archives of India, 1965.

Silver, Harold. *Education as History: Interpreting Nineteenth and Twentieth Century Education*. London: Methuen, 1983.

Simson, R. "Letter to the Secretary of the Government of India." 1869. *Selections from Educational Records of the Government of India: The Development of University Education 1860-87*. Ed. J.P. Naik. New Delhi: National Archives of India, 1963. 89–95.

Singh, S. and M.M. Bhalla, eds. *The Romance of Living*. Bombay: Orient Longman, 1962.

Sinha, Surendra Prasad. *English in India*. Patna: Janaki Prakashan, 1978.

Smith, Olivia. *The Politics of Language, 1791-1819*. Oxford: Clarendon, 1984.

Spivak, Gayatri Chakravorty. "Criticism, Feminism and the Institution." *The Postcolonial Critic: Interviews, Strategies Dialogues*. Ed. Sarah Harasum. New York: Routledge, 1990.

Srinivas, M.N. *Village, Caste, Gender and Method: Essays in Indian Social Anthropology*. New Delhi: Oxford UP, 1998.

Sriraman, T., ed. *College Prose*. Madras: Macmillan, 1989.

Sunder Rajan, Rajeswari, ed. *The Lie of The Land: English Literary Studies in India*. New Delhi: Oxford UP, 1993.

Tagore, Rabindranath. *Towards Universal Man*. Bombay: Asia, 1961.

Ten Tales for Indian Students. 1931. Bombay: Oxford UP, 1954.

Tharu, Susie, "The Arrangement of an Alliance: On the Making of English Literature." *Rethinking English: Essays in Literature, Language, History*. Ed. Svati Joshi. New Delhi: Trianka, 1991. 160–180.

_______. ed. *Subject to Change: Teaching Literature in the Nineties*. New Delhi: Orient Longman, 1998.

_______. "Chuni's Story." *Economic and Political Weekly* 33.46 (1998): 2916-7.

_______. and Tejaswini Niranjana. "Problems for a Contemporary Theory of Gender." *Social Scientist* 22.3-4 (1994): 93–117.

_______. and K. Lalita, ed. *Women Writing in India: 600 B.C. to the Present*.

New Delhi: Oxford UP, 1995. 2 vols.

Thibaut, G. "Letter to the Director of Public Instruction, North-Western Provinces on the Proposed University for the North-Western Provinces and Oudh." 1885. *Selections From Educational Records of the Government of India: The Development of University Education 1860-87.* Ed. J.P. Naik. New Delhi: National Archives of India, 1963. 405–418.

Thornley, G.C., ed. *Easier Scientific English Practice.* London: Longman, 1964.

Tickoo, M.L, H. Pant and S.K. Ram, eds. *On Top of the World: An Anthology of Contemporary Prose.* New Delhi: NCERT, 1978.

Tongue, R.K. and Shiv K. Kumar, eds. *An English Miscellany.* New Delhi: Oxford UP, 1981.

Trivedi, Harish and Meenakshi Mukherjee, eds. *Interrogating Post-Colonialism: Theory, Text and Context.* Shimla: Indian Institute of Advanced Study, 1996.

Vanikar, R.V. et al, eds. *Crossroads: A Guide to Communication in English.* Bombay: Oxford UP, 1992.

Varma, K.R. and E.C. Antony, eds. *Stories of Today.* Madras: Macmillan, 1981.

Vishnudev, P. and Tharakeshwar, V.B. "Dalits and Modernity: Few Notes on Dalit Literature, Dalits and English in the Post-colonial Space." Unpublished Paper.

Viswanathan, Gauri. *Masks of Conquest: Literary Study and British Rule in India.* London: Faber and Faber, 1989.

________. "English in a Literate Society." *The Lie of The Land: English Literary Studies in India.* Ed. Rajeswari Sunder Rajan. New Delhi: Oxford UP, 1993.

________. *Outside the Fold: Conversion, Modernity, and Belief.* New Delhi: Oxford UP, 1998.

Washbrook, David. "'To Each a Language of His Own': Language, Culture and Society in Colonial India." *Language, History and Class.* Ed. Penelope Corefield. Oxford: Basil Blackwell, 1991.

Wickramasinghe, Mira. "History Outside the Nation." *Economic and Political Weekly* 30.26 (1995): 1570-72.

Widdowson, Peter, ed. *Re-reading English.* London: Methuen, 1982.

Willinsky, John. *The New Literacy.* New York: Routledge, 1980.

Zaheer, Baber. *The Science of Empire: Scientific Knowledge, Civilization and Colonial Rule in India.* New Delhi: Oxford UP, 1998.

Index